W9-BNB-694

CONCILIUM
Religion in the Seventies

CONCILIUM, v. 97

EDITORIAL DIRECTORS:
BASIC EDITORIAL COMMITTEES: Roland Murphy and Bruce Vawter (Scripture) · Giuseppe Alberigo and Anton Weiler (Church History)

EDITORIAL COMMITTEES: *Group I: Christian Faith:* Edward Schille-beeckx and Bas van Iersel (Dogma)· Hans Küng and Walter Kasper (Ecumenism) · Johann Baptist Metz and Jean-Pierre Jossua (Funda-mental Theology) *Group II: Christian Ethics:* Franz Böckle and Jacques-Marie Pohier (Moral Theology) · Christian Duquoc and Casiano Floristán (Spirituality) · Andrew Greeley and Gregory Baum (Sociology of Religion) *Group III: The Practical Church:* Alois Müller and Norbert Greinacher (Pastoral Theology) · Herman Schmidt and David Power (Liturgy) · Peter Huizing and William Bassett (Canon Law)

EDITORIAL BOARD: Johann Baptist Metz · Jean-Pierre Jossua · Alfonso Alvarez Bolado · Jos Arntz · Paul Blanquart · Henri Bouillard · Werner Bröker · Daniel Callahan · Bertrand de Clercq · Joseph Comblin · Etienne Cornélis · Adolf Sarlap · Heimo Dolch · Albert Dondeyne · Dominique Dubarle · Iring Fetscher · Heinrich Fries · Giulio Girardi · Jean-Yves Jolif · Andreas van Melsen · Charles Moeller · Christopher Mooney · Maurice Nédoncelle · Willi Oelmüller · Francis O'Farrell · Raymond Panikkar · Norbert Schiffers · Heinz Schlette · Alexander Schwan · Juan Segundo · Robert Spaemann · David Tracy · Josef Trütsch · Roberto Tucci · Jan Walgrave · Bernhard Welte

THEOLOGICAL ADVISERS: Juan Alfaro · Marie-Dominique Chenu · Yves Congar · Gustavo Gutiérrez Merino · René Laurentin · Karl Rahner · Roberto Tucci

LAY SPECIALIST ADVISERS: Luciano Caglioti · August-Wilhelm von Eiff · Paulo Freire · Jean Ladrière · Pedro Lain Entralgo · Paul Ricoeur · Barbara Ward Jackson · Harald Weinrich

SECRETARY: Mlle Hanny Hendriks, Arksteestraat 3-5, Nijmegen, The Netherlands

New Series: Volume 7, Number 10: Canon Law

THE FUTURE OF THE RELIGIOUS LIFE

Edited by

Peter Huizing and William Bassett

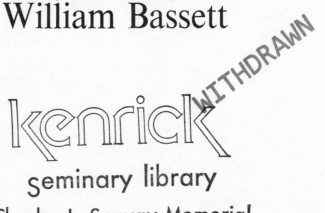

seminary library

Charles L. Souvay Memorial

WITHDRAWN

R
230.265
C744
V.97

761076

A CROSSROAD BOOK

The Seabury Press • New York

WITHDRAWN

The Seabury Press
815 Second Avenue
New York, N.Y. 10017

Copyright © 1974/5 by McGraw-Hill Inc. and Stichting Concilium. All rights reserved. No part of this book may be reproduced, stored in a retrieval system, or transmitted in any form or by any means, electronic, mechanical, photocopying, recording or otherwise, without the written permission of The Seabury Press.

Library of Congress Catalog Card Number: 76-10049
ISBN: 0-8164-2094-7
Printed in the United States of America

CONTENTS

Editorial: Some Guidelines

IT is obvious that this (umpteenth) crisis of growth in its history, which Christendom is undergoing at the moment, has particularly severe consequences for those groups that have chosen to identify the service of God with their life's work and their position in society.

Developments in the realm of religion and the Church can never be completely separated from developments in human society as a whole. Indeed, one of the marks of the crisis just now confronting mankind is the struggle to achieve much stronger bonds of solidarity and at the same time to assign much greater value to each person as an individual. Taken in and by themselves, these are not contradictions – quite the opposite. They are two inseparable aspects of one and the same process, so long as the point at issue is the mutual bond between them and the assessment of each on grounds of authentic human and authentic Christian values. But these values do not exist 'in themselves'. They are always embodied in particular forms of life, relations and structures; and so their realization is always merely relative. A state of crisis arises where there is a more and more marked awareness of certain aspects of that relativity, and a movement comes into action to break out of them in a development toward a further equilibrium. This is a continuous process, of course.

Now one of the characteristic features of the current crisis in the religious life – in a broad, idiomatic sense, not just in the strictly canonical one – is the tension between the traditional life-forms, relations and structures on the one hand, and on the other the urge, felt more powerfully at the personal level, to identify with a more socially, communally-oriented inspiration, derived from the Gospel.

This does not mean at all that the traditional forms of religious life, considered in themselves, are an obstacle to personal and communal inspiration. The history of the religious life is all too evident proof to the contrary. It is with good reason that monastic reform movements have again and again turned their back to the 'primitive account' of the founders and their friends as the prototype of authentic inspiration. Yet at the same time those reforms were also prompted by the arrival of ever new forms of religious life. The emergence of Cluny (910), of Citeaux (1098), of the regular canons (twelfth century), of the mendicant orders (thirteenth century), of the 'regular clergy' (sixteenth century), of the more recent congregations and communities of sisters, brothers and priests, of the secular institutes, has always had a side effect on the already existing religious communities, who found there the inspiration to adapt their traditions to the ever new demands of the age.

What this course of events does enshrine is a constant movement from an as complete as possible separation from the 'world' — the 'desert Fathers' — toward an advancing secularization, in the sense of positioning oneself more and more closely with and in the 'ordinary' life of society. Remarkably enough, this is at the same time a return to what are usually regarded as the oldest forms of Christian religious life. The 'virgins' and 'ascetics' in the earliest Christian communities were distinguished from the rest only by a more exclusive application on their part to such expressions of zeal as prayer and fasting and to acts of service in the congregation. They did not live apart and had no special distinguishing marks. Progressive developments have always been set going by small, spontaneously constituted groups which then often grew with extraordinary speed. In the spontaneous groups now springing up all over the place a number of shifts of emphasis with regard to tradition are again noticeable. In place of the heavy stress on obedience to individual superiors, a greater sense of solidarity among all the members comes to the fore. Eschewing private property and income is less important than personal frugality in living.

When it comes to accommodation and 'life style' the idea is to fit in with the classes who live plainest of all, without any need to be distinguished from them in this or that way. Although most elect to remain unmarried, still this is often not a condition for belonging to the group; and various groups have both male and female members. As regards the life of the group and the shape assigned to it, a considerable degree of personal freedom is allowed to the individual. In the matter of work there is a preference for tasks that will assist those sections of the population most in need of help; but even there the choice, as a rule, is left to the members. Nobody holds a special position within the groups, not even those members who are priests. For the present, at any rate, the aim is not to extend the group; rather the opposite. Participation in a large community, in which most people are not personally known to one another, is felt to be an unreal abstraction. So far there has been no need for canonical recognition on the part of ecclesiastical authority.

Parallels to these changes of emphasis are equally operative, however, in the 'old' religious communities. Of their members a fairly considerable number are actually living in mixed spontaneous groups. But many others are coming to put less store by the outward forms of the tradition. What they feel to be the central core of their existence is an undivided commitment to their belief in the mystery of the dying and living of Jesus; so that allegiance to a particular community and a particular life-style is seen as an expression of that commitment, which itself cannot exist without manifest expression and symbolism; but in so far as it entails obligations toward people, within the church community as well as the religious group, these are not on the same level as the commitment to the Christ-mystery, undertaken before God. People would prefer to hear no more flights of language, for instance, about authorities who occupy the place of Christ or who by virtue of the promise of obedience hand out their orders, because the obligation towards them cannot be identified with the essential core of the religious vows. This in itself has consequences for thought about religious authority, dispensations from vows, the validity assigned to professions, and so on. 'Blind' obedience gives way to participation by everyone in decision-making. Large communities get merged into small functional affiliations. People aim at an obviously frugal and plain sort of existence to which they themselves give a shape and in which they bear responsibility for the outlay of resources. There is a trend toward abandoning large institutions and enterprises for social and developmental work among the most needy. Doing away with differences in rank, based on ordination or solmen profession, has already been generally accepted, as well as the giving up of detailed rules for the personal religious life, where much more self-reliance is called for.

The working out of this process is of course not free of crises — and grave ones at that. Many find the challenge of a more personal and self-reliant way of living out a religious inspiration too much for them. For a lot of others the pressure on their personal aspirations of excessively slow development within their own group is too great to bear. As a result not only are there mass defections, but acute tensions arise among those who for the time being remain. The group's uncertainties about its own life and work can lay a heavy burden on its morale.

This number is intended to be a modest contribution to reflection about what goes on in the current crisis affecting the religious life; and that, on the basis of past experiences and of thinking about fundamental values of the religious life and its place in the church structures, as well as in the context of current experiences and expectations. The idea of this is not to get a tighter grip on developments or lay down directives as to what should happen now. Just the opposite, in fact. The rise and growth of the various trends and movements in religion have never been due to official measures and organizations, but always to free, personal inspiration. Starting from the theological fact of the religious vocation, it could not be otherwise — and must always remain so. The religious themselves cannot resolve their problems by an appeal to authority but only through their own honest-to-goodness inspiration. Even the comments of church officials in their addresses, not meant to be rules so much as pious reflections, regarding for example the religious habit or the closure of a monastery or the question of house-sharing or the practice of confession and that kind of thing, may in gatherings such as provincial and general chapters completely frustrate a down-to-earth exchange of ideas, if a group blocks it by an appeal to such pronouncements on the part of *the* church authority, which leaves the others totally at a loss what to do.

The various contributions give some ground for justifiable optimism. Admittedly, the numbers of religious continue to get smaller at the present time. One must even come to terms with the very sad fate of groups who can see their end approaching; and that really is not always through culpable spiritual decline. Then too it is inevitable that the new paths being taken by the religious life should be paths of personal suffering for many, and for many wholly impassable; so that the motives and springs of action may well be diametrically opposed. One can only hope that the religious inspiration will prove strong enough for people to go on having faith in one another and supporting one another, even if they cannot yet understand one another.

But there is absolutely no solid reason to suppose that the life of religion has finally had its day. This is equally true, for that matter, of the great schools of spirituality in religion. The Benedictine, Augustinian, Franciscan, Domincan, Bernardine, Ignatian, Theresian and countless other gospel-inspired sources of renewed spiritual life have already survived so many crises, some of which at any rate have certainly been not less severe than those of today. The already quite evident symptoms of a more powerfully felt gospel-based inspiration both in new groups and in older ones justify the hope that the source from which they all derive and on which they draw will once again supply its living water.

PETER HUIZING
WILLIAM BASSETT

Translated by H. Hoskins

Walter Dirks

The Monks' Response

IN considering the 'response' which holy monks have given I shall here be taking the word in Toynbee's sense of a response to a challenge.

I

Considering this aspect in relation to particular founders of religious orders will enable us to exclude in advance other dimensions of monastic existence. Among these are the commitment to the 'counsels' or appeals of Jesus, which have come down to us in the tradition as the three vows of 'perfect poverty', 'perfect obedience', and complete abstinence from human erotic and sexual potential. These vows are a commitment to a way of life which strives for a typical perfection and is shaped by its image. Also excluded is consideration of whether there is a characteristically monastic spirituality and detailed examination of specifically Benedictine, Franciscan, Dominican or Jesuit styles of piety.

Leaving out all these aspects is not intended as a comment on their significance for the individual monk, for the community of monks, or for the Church and its history. Another element, however, which is basic to most orders (though not for hermits and hardly for the Carthusians), the common life, will prove to be significant in the 'response' of the monks. On the other hand, its importance does not lie only, and often not even primarily, in this response; it has roots also outside our challenge-response model. It would have made no real difference to the tradition if a fourth vow of brotherly life had been added to the familiar three.

But motivation is important to our enquiry when it is not directed at one of the previously mentioned elements of monastic life, but instead at the 'challenge', at a particular social and historical situation which has the character of a challenge. It may happen that a Christian remains alone in his recognition of a situation and his attempt to respond to it. Joan of Arc and Nicholas of Flüe are perhaps 'founders manqué' of this sort. These two fifteenth-century saints found the Christian answer to very specific challenges in their political situations, those of the French-Lorraine frontier areas at the time of the Hundred Years' War at the beginning of the century and the crisis in the Swiss confederation on domestic and foreign policy two generations later. I venture to call their motivations Christian because of the real connexion with real neighbours and because of the complete abandonment to God's will and the person of Jesus which is a constant feature of the responses of these two saints.

But my subject is 'monks', and I must therefore limit these thoughts to the situations, motivations and actions of responsible saints who found or formed an understanding of the challenge and their response in others and so created disciples in their spirit.

The approach I have adopted presupposes the existence in the founders of religious orders of a historical outlook or at least historical sensitivity: in three ways. The challenge came from the 'world': the world of nations and states, of society. The response matches the state of that world and seeks to alter it in the spirit of Christ. A static and unhistorical consciousness lacks the imagination which sees the relevance of the present as the result of a historical past and the chance of a new future. In other words, at the centre of these founders' work must have been a breaking of the Graeco-Roman limitations imposed on the Christian intellectual tradition since the destruction of Jewish Christianity between 70 and 123, and a rediscovery of the Jewish-Christian prophetic factor suppressed in that destruction. This was the product of historical consciousness, although it was certainly not often understood as such. The fact that in the process the could understand, or had a feeling for, actual earthly society and its historical dimension also establishes a relationship with the prophetic tradition of Judaism. They saw things in the world and saw them as changeable and in need of change; they began to open a new chapter of world history. At the same time, however, they saw or felt salvation and the saving institution of the Church in a more historical way than their contemporaries. They believed that Christianity as Christianity, the Church as the Church, was capable of change, of a new future. The third historical aspect is the unhindered and natural unity of the first two aspects, those of secular history and saving history. Again like the prophets of the Old Covenant, they saw no difference between rescuing the people and rescuing God's covenant with that people through a renewal of both in one. Obviously much of this motivation will have been unconscious. To have a sense of history is quite different from being able to handle the categories of a theory of history developed much later; it does not mean having an explicit historical consciousness.

I implied earlier that I would choose four examples: Benedict and his disciples, Francis and his brothers, Dominic and his companions, Ignatius and his comrades. To avoid misunderstandings I must make it clear here that of course what I have excluded from consideration can and indeed must have the character of a 'response' to a call from God. Saints do not act on their own intiative; they are called, whatever the form in the particular case. This article is only about a particular form of response, the call to respond to a historical challenge.

II

Benedict's explicit motivation was limited to the internal life of the Church. Though he himself had begun by spending a number of years as a hermit in seclusion, in his polemic against the wandering single monks he not only declared himself in favour of the cenobitic, or common monastic, life but stiffened its underlying principle by adding the requirement of *stabilitas loci*. His monks were to spend their whole lives in the monastery they had chosen. But monks were not the only people who went wandering at that time. The period which had not yet ended when Benedict, after long (and sometimes bitter) experiences with all sorts of monasteries and monks, drew up his rules for Monte Cassino in 530 was that of the great migrations known as the 'barbarian invasions'. If we relate Benedict's basic rules directly to the conditions of the time, many of them show a specific point and context. *Stabilitas loci* is not just a monastic principle, but a slogan for a whole period: give up wandering and campaigning and settle in one place. The Benedictine *pax* does not apply just to the heart of the monk and his life with his brethren, but to the whole violence-ridden age. The migrations had produced a mingling of peoples and classes, but there were still different laws for the Romans and the Germanic lords, and even more for free men and slaves. Benedict's Christian answer was: 'All are welcome among us; these distinctions, including that of race, do not exist in the monastery.' His famous motto, *Ora et labora*, the combination of prayer and work, did not apply to the much later Benedictine intellectual work, but to agriculture and manufacture; it was this which was to be accompanied by prayer. The beginnings of Roman clericalism, rooted in the Constantinian symbiosis of Church and state, were ignored: there was to be at least one priest in the community so that the eucharist could be celebrated, and for the same reason the community was to produce wine. It is impossible to find the role of the priest in his religious community more austerely stated than this. The economically self-sufficient community was not to defend itself.

The austerity and organizational skill of Benedict of Nursia have rightly been seen and praised as an inheritance of Rome, but it should not be forgotten that this was the founding of a Christian self-sufficient collective farm which had no Roman models. His monastery was an agricultural and manufacturing commune — with the only exception of celibacy. It is an alternative model to that of the early medieval economy and society which culminated in the power of the sword, feudal hierarchy and the threefold division into the power of the lords, the bondage of the peasants and lower officials and prayer by proxy in the monastery. I oversimplify, of necessity, but is it wrong to see Benedict's fraternal monastic farm as the model of a Christian Middle Ages which never was? The model was not adopted because society and Church did not understand and did not accept Benedict's answer to the challenge of the migrations. This Christian Middle Ages would have been a network of Christian collective farms. When Benedict's response to the situation at the end of the period of the migrations was not taken up, but channelled into an order — a typical process, as we shall see — there still remained a great cultural achievement, but anyone who is not a determinist will also have to accept that this diversion was one of the reasons why the Christian society rejected Benedict's offer. The Benedictine *pax* remained a compensation for knightly glorification of the sword, for constant feuding and feudal subordination.

III

The stigmatic saint of Alverna, who fought so desperately against any institutionalization of his evangelical appeal to Christians and Christianity, is an unlikely symbol for a 'response' to 'challenges' from society. And yet in fact he shows this particular aspect with unusual clarity.

The poor man of Assisi was sent not to the poor, but to the rich. We hear nothing of alms-giving in Franciscan circles: the brothers begged only for themselves. They did not even pick up coins lying in the street to give to the next poor person. Francis told them to leave the money in the dirt. This typifies his relationship to money. Francis was the son of a rich cloth merchant. He lived in the period and the country in which banking was beginning to develop. For a thousand years the Church had tried to ban interest by legal and disciplinary measures, but had not been able to. (Even in the middle of the nineteenth century papal pronouncements dealt with the permissibility of interest.) In Francis money was opposed not by a law, but by a man. He did not mobilise the poor against the new rich, like others before him, but lived among the rich and lived and prayed against them — more precisely, against a new form of money, or one which was entering on a new importance. Previously, wealth had been created by agricultural work or mnaufacture, to a much lesser extent through exchange, by advantage gained in dealing and bargaining. It was acquired by inheritance or victory in battle; its symbol was gold and ornaments, and the money produced out of the gold was a means of exchange. It was also, however, as money lent, 'loans', a direct source of new money — even though in theory the principle was maintained that 'Money cannot breed money'. In the early Middle Ages a double transformation of quantity into quality was beginning to take place: trade was becoming more important than production, and trade in money became autonomous in the banking system. The process was unavoidable, and must even be seen as beneficial unless we want to revoke retrospectively Europe's development into an industrial society. What Francis clearly felt was the greater inferiority of the new money of trade and banking. Regarded instrumentally, the new wealth was more abstract than the old, which had been tied to land, houses, equipment, ornaments and gold. From the point of view of people, it was anything but abstract; it was very subjective. It was to be expected that it would take a stronger hold on the movements and powers of the heart than the more innocent old material possessions acquired by work, elementary forms of trade, inheritance or war. In later imperial Rome there had already been 'speculators', but in the harsh times of the invasions and the early Middle Ages the type disappeared. Now it re-emerged in more substantial form, and it also became legitimate. Living on the difference between the money value of goods bought and goods sold was the foundation of the house in which the young Francis grew up. He became the poor saint of the rich. It is only by realizing this that we can see why he did not regard himself as having discovered a special way of life, rather than simply the way of the gospel, which he regarded as the rule for all Christians. It is part of this outlook that he should immediately call women into his movement, and that finally in his own lifetime the 'third order' was set up for the married. It was in this body, which later degenerated into a pious confraternity, that the Franciscan movement was to have developed its true historical significance. But it was not Fugger, but Elizabeth of Thuringia, who became a tertiary. The lady of the poor is a lovable saint, but she is also a sign that the historical meaning of the Franciscan response to the challenge of 'money in itself' had not been understood. To be poor in spirit as a producer, salesman or even a banker, to work and earn in that spirit and develop structures which would have allowed the men of a different modern age to become Christians, that was the idea which the centuries after Francis failed to turn into reality.

Here again channelling into an order was a compensation for what failed to happen. Just as the bold lords of the high Middle Ages sent their second or third sons into abbeys to do victorious prayer and penance, the second and third sons of the merchants became friars minor. On the other hand, it should be noted that while the mendicant orders failed to understand the first brother's response, did not take it up and, above all, were unable to pass on the crucial elements of it, they did perform a service to the kingdom of God in a totally different way, as friends of the poor.

IV

If the reader has grasped the point of these two models, the meaning of the following short sketches should be clear.

The Dominicans were preachers related most closely perhaps to the Franciscans, and their distinctive feature is perhaps best seen in the point on which Francis opposed them, their reverence for learning (starting with theology and philosophy). They were the men who, as 'God's freethinkers', with the help of the new access to the more sober thought of the Greeks, recently made available by the Arabs, broke the ban of the 'School', of sacred and untouchable tradition, of what was in the books. The fact that they themselves became a school, that their ideas have become known as 'scholasticism', is an irony of intellectual history. To reach the centre of events we must concentrate not on the founder himself, but on his immediate disciple, St Thomas Aquinas. Particularly fruitful intellectual work (and great intellectual existence) can sometimes be achieved by drawing together the whole of the past and at the same time drawing out the seed of the future. The names Hegel, Marx and Goethe can stand for a later synthesis and programme combined, and Aquinas's importance was that he combined the wisdom of the Western Fathers and that of Aristotle and his Arab and Jewish commentators with a fresh feeling for the Gospel, and yet in the originality of many of his ideas became the first modern philosopher. That this work at the end of his life seemed to him to be 'straw' completes the picture: the first modern philosopher was a Christian. It makes no difference to this fact that he dragged this or that awkward remnant of traditional narrow-mindedness with him, that he could not jump from his time into the twentieth century, nor that he is not an isolated figure, but has predecessors and contemporaries. Nor is his status affected by the way his disciples have kept more to the *verba magistri* than to his example of bold and methodical intellectual exploration; he himself was very early the Christian answer to the challenge of the awakening European mind.

V

We are inclined these days to be suspicious of St Ignatius's absolute devotion to the pope. Nevertheless that too embodies a liberation from an intolerable burden of small and medium and greater lords, the huge double pyramid of graduated dependence which oppressed the Christian individual ecclesiastically and politically. This extreme reliance on the pope meant more freedom from the parish priest, bishop and prince-bishop, from the court, the city authorities and the prince. The immediate connexion with the pope concealed an immediate connexion with God. The Counter-Reformation, though in many places perhaps even more brutal than a Reformation which was itself imposed by secular power, was more closely related to its opposite than is often supposed. There can be argument about the wisdom of the Jesuits' policy of attaching themselves to key figures and élites rather than the masses, but in their own particular way they championed the freedom of the Christian man in the Catholic world as much as Luther in his more radical approach, and like him they based freedom on obedience to conscience. For all his disciplined and militant attitude, in the parts of Europe which remained Catholic, Ignatius provided a response to the challenge of emancipation in Church politics and secular politics. Like the leaders of the enlightenment, he stands for the destruction of the medieval pyramid of authority. However much the absolute obedience he swore to the pope helped to fix the Catholic system for several centuries in a rigid defensive attitude, it is many modern Jesuits who are showing the true meaning of this tie, to educate Catholics into mature Christians. Even in the modernist controversy, some took one side and some the other – a result of the ambivalence of that identification with the pope. Today, however, it is becoming increasingly clear that their response to the challenge of intellectual emanicpation is essentially personal conscience – in the context of the people of God and the Gospel.

VI

These brief remarks must end with an apology. This article set out to trace a particular historical development (which meant ignoring many opposite factors) and to describe ideal types. It has not tried to present the whole truth about the response function of monks, but to sketch a single aspect.

Translated by Francis McDonagh

David Knowles

The Rise and Decline of Cluny

THE great monastic family which took its name from the Burgundian abbey of Cluny, and grew to form a network that included more than a thousand houses great and small, offers the historian a spectacle of numerical and institutional growth, religious and ecclesiastical influence, and political and sociological importance without parallel in the Middle Ages before the mid-twelfth century.[1] Cluny reached this position in the epoch when Europe was rising from the aftermath of the barbarian invasions, by way of feudalism, to organized monarchical government, and from a church in the hands of lay lords to one in which the spirituality (that is, the clerical order in all its grades) secured freedom from lay control and, in return, claimed supreme authority in the person of the pope. The Cluniac body can be studied therefore either as a reservoir of spiritual and ecclesiastical power, or as an active part of society, or as a purely monastic institute. In all these aspects it can be isolated for examination to a degree impossible in the religious bodies of the later Middle Ages, when multiple relationships of all kinds confuse the picture.

For the purposes of this article, the limiting dates will be 909, the foundation-date of Cluny, and 1156, when Peter the Venerable, the last great abbot of Cluny, died and, in the words of Mabillon, Cluny lost its pristine splendour, which it was never to regain in full measure.[2]

Cluny was founded only a century after the synod of Aachen (817), held by Charlemagne's son and successor, Lewis the Pious, at which the reforming abbot, Benedict of Aniane, imposed unity of observance under the Rule of St Benedict on all the monasteries of the Empire. This unity dissolved rapidly with the break-up of the Carolingian em-

17

pire, the disintegration of overhead government in western Europe, and the feudalization of society. Abbeys fell under the control of the lord or bishop who had founded them, or in whose territory they lay.

Cluny had the good fortune to be situated in virtually independent territory, and to be guaranteed freedom from molestation at the hands of bishops or secular lords by its unusually full and explicit charter of foundation,[3] but its remarkable expansion was due to its good fortune in having a long succession of eminent and saintly abbots, who inspired their own subjects with zeal and attracted others to make benefactions, bestow spiritual favours and solicit union. Between 909 and 1156 (247 years) Cluny had only nine abbots, one of whom ruled for only five months, while the four greatest between them covered 180 years. In this long story Odo, though in office for a relatively brief period (962-942), set the course the abbey was to pursue; Odilo (994-1048) did more than any other to develop and plan the Cluniac 'order', while Hugh the Great, in his reign of sixty years (1048-1109), saw an enormous expansion of both the network and of the mother-house, and was responsible for the great basilica (Cluny III) and the provision of adequate monastic buildings. To Peter the Venerable (1122-56) it fell to hold the fort and repair the breaches when Cluny's paramountcy was threatened by domestic disturbances, economic distress, and widespread symptons of decay.

The great family of Cluny's filiations and dependencies gave her a unique and supreme position in the monastic world of the eleventh and early twelfth centuries. The number of her subjects and allies is still a matter of controversy, but they must certainly have numbered more than a thousand, even if small priories and cells are excluded. The core consisted of direct foundations from Cluny and their filiations, often to the third or fourth generation. Then came the numerous monasteries reformed by abbots of Cluny. Some of these remained abbeys, others were reduced to the rank of priories; some were allowed to elect their superiors, others received those appointed by the abbot of Cluny. Some houses were entirely controlled by Cluny; others accepted its observance, but were otherwise independent. Finally there were abbeys outside the Cluniac network, who elected or received a Cluniac abbot (Reading was an English instance), while yet others did no more than accept a large part of the customs of Cluny.

As Cluny herself derived many of her liturgical and domestic usages from monasteries of the Carolingian reform, there was a family resemblance between almost all the black monk abbeys of western Europe in the eleventh century, and the term Cluniac was used in England and elsewhere as synonymous with black monk. Such a widening of the term Cluniac deprived it of its proper meaning, but it serves to remind us how powerful the image of Cluny had become. While a majority of the houses of the order were in what is modern France, Spain, also Portugal, Italy, Germany, Flanders and England had numerous member houses.

All those belonging to monasteries controlled by Cluny made their profession to the abbot of Cluny, and were counted as members of the chapter of Cluny if they visited the mother-house. As for the abbot of Cluny, he spent most of his time travelling round his scattered family, receiving their vows and reforming their discipline, or dealing with their affairs at Cluny or Rome. Cluny never attempted, in the period we are considering, to devise any system of devolution or sharing of power. Her 'order' was regarded simply as a large family, an extension of Cluny herself. There were other such 'orders' or groups, that of Bec, for example. The analogy to a feudal 'honour', a group of separate estates granted by the king to a tenant-in-chief who had sub-tenants beneath him, was never made explicitly by Cluny, but it is valid within limits, for the act of submission and its conditions were contained in a charter, and the profession to the abbot of Cluny resembled the act of homage of a feudal tenant to his lord, while the chapter at Cluny could be looked upon as a parallel to the council of tenants assembled by the king, to give advice and to hear and accept his decrees.

No attempt was made before the thirteenth century to draw up or impose a constitutional framework for the whole family. Such a task would have been impossible; it would be anachronistic to expect it. The charters of dependence implied an acceptance of all the customs and liturgical arrangements of Cluny, but there were no horizontal links between the various Cluniac houses, and no chapter of the whole order at which discipline and legislation could be considered. All houses, however, shared all Cluny's papal and other privileges, including that of exemption when it came.

The bonds of the family were therefore threefold. First, there was the personal submission of each monk to the abbot of Cluny by virtue of his vow. Next, there was the acceptance by each house of the Rule of St Benedict as interpreted by the Uses of Cluny. Thirdly, the charter of dependence imposed the recognition of certain obligations and sanctioned certain privileges and immunities.

Historians have emphasized that Cluny at her foundation was guaranteed freedom from all external interference and placed under the ownership and protection of the Apostles Peter and Paul in Rome. This should be understood in the context of its age, which was an age of lordship, feudalism and the proprietary church. 'Spiritual things', that is, churches, abbeys and their various possessions and revenues, were regarded as radically belonging to their founders or the lord of the land, or the secular lords to whom they had commended themselves, whether kings, or regional dukes, or smaller landowners. In times of stress or decay a lord might invade or confiscate monastic revenues, and as owners of an abbey (*abbatia*) they often ousted the abbot, replacing him by a prior. They could demand services and exact taxes, both occasional and regular. If the bishop were lord he could use the church for ordinations and other occasions, burden the community by his visits, and organize or disorganize their life. In the tenth century it was not a question of ecclesiastical interference or control; the whole of the external fabric of the church rested on lordship and ownership. Cluny's original freedom lay in the realm of lordship and commendation, and it was secured by commendation to the Apostle Peter represented by the reigning pope, whose only demand was a small annual fee (*census*).

A great change came when the reviving and reforming papacy began to exploit its resources, and to revive and reinterpret old canonical powers and rights. The full pre-history of 'exemption', that is, the exclusion of the jurisdiction of the diocesan bishop, in favour of direct control by the papacy, has yet to be elucidated in detail, but the liberation of a monastery from the control of the local Ordinary in his spiritual capacity dates from the eleventh century and the era of the reformed papacy. The papal claims were buttressed by early canonical decrees, authentic and forged, and were at first resisted by bishops using the same canonical collections. Thus the bishops, like the papacy, were concerned to reassert rights bestowed by councils of the early church, particularly those of Chalcedon. For this reason the French bishops, among them the bishop of Macon in whose diocese Cluny lay, were active against the monks. This brought about increased papal activity in asserting the rights of the monks, and from the last decade of the tenth century onwards successive popes issued to Cluny and some other houses permission to choose any bishop for ordination and consecration, and in 1024 John XIX freed Cluny from all episcopal control, and subjected the abbey directly to the Holy See. This was challenged as contravening ancient legislation throughout the provinces of Vienne and Lyons, and finally the bishop of Macon appeared at Cluny with armed supporters to demand the right of preaching there and the use of monastic buildings (1063), while some years later the archbishop of Lyons interdicted Cluniac churches and excommunicated their priests (1079). The bishops in so doing precipitated a decisive move by Gregory VII, who confirmed all privileges given in the past by popes to Cluny, and in the council of 1080 asserted her absolute liberty under the Apostolic See, a privilege applicable to all her foundations and dependencies.[4] This declaration of Gregory VII was decisive. Had the pope shown himself neutral, the bishops might well have curtailed Cluny's activities and thus deprived the papacy of a great corps of supporters in its struggle for supremacy.

What was the secret of Cluny's success and prestige? Many circumstances and causes have been suggested. Her position in territory near, but not controlled by, the French and German monarchs, and near, but not actually upon, the great highway carrying traffic from Italy to Paris and England doubtless had its influence. Other new orders, including Citeaux, had their cradle nearby. But the real causes must lie deeper. Cluny's clear and practical programme of the monastic life, though a necessary condition of its success, is not a sufficient explanation, nor is the foundation charter. Other houses had similar advantages. Cluny's success was primarily due to her series of saintly, eminent, and richly gifted abbots, mostly of high birth, all possessed of wide sympathies and diplomatic skill, all with a genius for missionary activity, and all preaching a single form of the monastic life, that of the Rule interpreted with human sympathy and a liturgical bias, within the context of a feudal and aristocratic society. Moreover, Cluny's age of expansion coincided with the earliest phase of European adolescence, when the monastic life was regarded primarily in its social aspects as a sure and honourable means of salvation and an essential element in the life of Christendom, an 'estate' of prayer within the common life. Cluny stood for an ascesis that was at once traditional and yet within the physical and psychological capability of a normally healthy man. So doing, she attracted vocations from all parts, including a large number of well-born recruits, and never lacked monks of real holiness of life: the great abbots themselves, those she sent out as bishops, private monks such as Ulrich of Zell, priors outside Cluny such as Lanzo of Lewes, and, in darker days, the examples of holiness recorded among his contemporaries by Peter the Venerable. Peter himself was an epitome of the best Cluniac qualities.

Nevertheless Cluny, like other celebrated abbeys, passed through the seasons of spring blossom, summer fruit, and autumnal decay. If her fame was at its height under Hugh the Great around 1050-80, there was a clear decline at the end of the eleventh century, showing outwardly in the abbacy of Pons (1109-1122). Many causes have been found for this, some external, others internal. It has been the fate of most successful bodies to be ruined by their very success. Cistercians and Franciscans were to go the same way. Then Cluny was wealthy. Wealth has always been the bane of monastic life, and Cluny suffered both from affluence and from anxiety when her economy became insecure. Success brought recruits in flocks. Under Hugh numbers grew from 100 to 300, and under Peter reached nearly 400. This caused serious physical and psychological strain. Similarly, in the order outside the walls of Cluny, the vast numbers were unmanageable. The strength of the system had lain in the firm control and guidance of a single abbot such as Odilo or Hugh, but towards the end of Hugh's reign the task was too much even for a great ruler who was also a saint.

Like the Roman empire, Cluny's huge edifice collapsed under its own weight. *Ipsa mole ruit sua.*

There were other causes, visible even if more spiritual. There was at Cluny in Hugh's last years a failure to test vocations and train recruits. There was no minimum time, let alone a mandatory year, between the clothing of a novice and his monastic profession. A single day was considered sufficient. The Cluniacs, along with many others, had departed from one of the most valuable regulations of St Benedict, which now has long been a canonical obligation, the year-long noviciate with its tests and training. This practice at Cluny was partly due to the prevailing view of the monastic profession as a second baptism, an earnest of salvation, open to all as a refuge from disaster. Hence at Cluny the novice, if he desired, could make his profession almost at once.[5]

Yet another cause of decline was the over-emphasis laid on the liturgical element in the monastic life. The Divine Office, which in the Rule of St Benedict and other early rules was only one element, albeit the most important, of the monk's daily occupations, had received so many accretions of prayers, Offices and elaborations of chant and ceremonial, that it had come to fill an inordinate proportion of the waking hours. Contemporaries noted the fatigue caused by long spells of chanting, and by the time taken by the large numbers to execute ceremonies and processions.[6] Not only was time short for private prayer and reading, but physical work had all but disappeared as part of the monastic life.

Finally, and most deeply, Cluny's ideal of the monastic life was beginning to lose its appeal in the changing Europe.[7] The monastery of the Rule of St Benedict was a small household of men apart from the world who prayed, read and worked together in the service of Christ. Two centuries later the typical monastery had become larger, and the monks, now mostly in priestly orders and occupied in liturgical service, were regarded as refugees from the evils of life, secure in the ark of salvation. Now, in the eleventh century, many of the finest spirits of the age saw as the only remedy in evil times a life more severe and intense than the busy, liturgical life of a large abbey. The life of a hermit, in penance and prayer, appealed widely and took shape in institutes such as the Camaldulese and Carthusians.[8] This was the beginning of a return to the primitive conception of the monastic life, no longer seen as an 'estate' or intercessory body, but as an individual call to serve Christ in poverty and hardship, in a laborious and simple life. The final answer to the call of the spirit of the age was the 'new monastery' of Citeaux. There, a small group, with firm resolve and drastic consistency, attacked by implication Cluniac ideals and practice all along the line. They replace the immense abbey and her multitudinous family under a single abbot by small (at first) abbeys joined together not by a detailed, legal charter on a feudal model, but by a short document calculated to preserve the original spirit of the first fathers of Citeaux, the Charter of Love (*Carta Caritatis*). The monarch of the Cluniac empire was replaced by a meeting of all the abbots once a year, on an absolute equality, to take decisions for all. The diffuse and ponderous Uses of Cluny were replaced by the Rule understood and followed literally, and the crowds at Cluny were replaced by a solitary site and the spirit of the desert. The spirit of the world was conjured by a renunciation of all revenues and services. Lay lords and bishops were kept at a distance, and the houses were founded in desolate localities, which were converted into fields, meadows and orchards by the labours of the monks themselves. The Divine Office was shorn of its accretions, and diet, sleep and silence were regulated by the Rule. The year-long novitiate was strictly observed. The practice of accepting oblate children was discontinued, and the multitude of servants who filled Cluny with noise, insulting the monks and filching the provisions, were excluded; the monks cooked and cleaned for themselves. When fields and animals required more time than the monks could give, lay-brothers (*conversi*) who lived a quasi-monastic life apart from the choir monks were received to perform all the heavy tasks. A few years later, under the influence of St Bernard, a frontal attack was made on Cluniac luxury and exuberant sculptures and precious objects in large churches, and for a time the Cistercians showed a puritanical severity.

In all these ways the Cistercians were silent critics, but a few decades after 1100 the criticism became vocal, indeed strident, when Bernard delivered his first broadside,[9] attacking Cluny with all the force of his piety and rhetoric. His genius and his reputation shook the defences of Cluny, and have ever since continued to give ammunition to her critics. Many of his strictures were just and unanswerable, as his great antagonist, Peter the Venerable, tacitly admitted by publishing in 1132 a long series of disciplinary articles some of which were directly aimed at abuses catalogued by Bernard. On some points, however, such as the short novitiate, he held firm, and he asserted with eloquence the Cluniac ideal of moderation and charity, and of the right and duty of Christians to beautify the house of God.

Recent criticism has tended to approve the case made out by Peter. But to most contemporaries the Cistercians seemed, at least for fifty years, to stand for a simpler, purer and more bracing monastic life than that of the large and rich abbeys of the Cluniacs and other black monks. As a matter of history, it was not the Cluniacs, but the more balanced regime of the Norman and Anglo-Norman monasteries, such as Bec and St Albans, that became the most powerful rivals of the Cistercians in later centuries. Bec, not Cluny, was the ancestor of Solesmes and Beuron. Nevertheless, to contemporaries in the early decades of the twelfth century, the image of Cluny remained imposing. Urban II, and probably also Paschal II, were Cluniac popes, and Cluniacs were used as legates and appointed to leading bishoprics. There is some evidence that young monks who were well-born and promising were, as the phrase goes, 'groomed' for a high career, either up the Cluniac ladder of promotion, or at the papal court. Monks of Cluny were still demanded or imposed as abbots outside the Cluniac network, and fifty years after the foundation of Citeaux Cluny was still regarded as one of the pillars of the Church.[10]

The relationship between Cluny and the Gregorian reform has been a topic of controversy during the past hundred years. The reigning opinion during the nineteenth century was that the monastic revival, of which Cluny was the eminent leader, led gradually to the papalistic movement of the eleventh century and to the Gregorian Reform. Fifty years ago historians turned their attention to the new austere, erimitical, trend in north Italy, and to the reforming monasticism of Lorraine which, as the homeland of Leo IV and Humbert of Moyenmoutier, was seen as a cradle of reform. More recently still, the place of Cluny in the movement has been once more emphasized. It is now generally agreed that the basis of the reform was moral and spiritual, led by monks and directed towards giving to the world the only recipe known to them, the monastic ideal. Gregory VII was in full accord with this, but looked upon a reformed and powerful papacy as the God-given agency for the renewal of the Church. Himself a monk, he accepted the monastic order as an existing ally, already favoured by all the popes of his lifetime, which he would strengthen by multiple favours. Circumstances, as has been seen, had brought Cluny into conflict with bishops, and Gregory asserted his paramount authority by conferring on her complete exemption from all authority save that of the Holy See.[11] This absolute liberty was the supreme achievement of papal power, and in return Cluny supported papal policy in Spain from Sahagun, and in the German lands from Schaffhausen.

Hugh the Great, known to all medievalists as the peacemaker at Canossa, was throughout his later life a firm supporter of Gregorian aims, though his noble birth and personal character, together with his wide European connexions, made of him a central, though not a compromising, diplomat. Cluny, with so many sons of the aristocratic families of Euope among its community and dependents, was conservative in outlook and sympathy, but Hugh and his monks knew what they owed to the papacy, while for Gregory VII Cluny was the supreme example of papal protection and power. The pope did not exaggerate when he wrote that he and Abbot Hugh were walking the same way with an identical outlook and spirit.[12]

Cluny has sometimes been credited with a part in preparing the minds of men for the crusades.[13] Such evidence as exists tells against any suggestion of direct propaganda, but indirectly they were involved in the pilgrimage to Compostela and the war of reconquest in Spain, which undoubtedly helped to familiarize French knights and barons with the conception of pilgrimage as a means of remission of sin, and with the holy war as a service of the papacy. The link between the two ideas was supplied by Urban II, not by Cluny, but there is evidence that Cluny encouraged its friends to take the cross of the crusader.

A final word may be said on the architecture and sculpture of Cluny.[14] The great basilica of Abbot Hugh (Cluny III), which has justly been called the masterpiece of late romanesque and of monastic architecture, had a very great influence on other Cluniac churches, great or small, in contemporary France, as had also lesser churches, such as Vezelay and Lewes, on churches in their neighbourhood. Similarly, the sculptures that adorned Cluny III were influential both in style and iconography. Indeed, the excavations and studies of Dr. K. J. Conant have gone far to establish Cluny's position as the source of the style that spread all over central and southern France. As for the pilgrimage to Compestella, its origins and development are still uncertain. Did Cluny make or accept foundations in order to encourage the pilgrimage, or did she simply use existing houses to meet the needs of a pilgrimage already established? Whatever answer is given to this question, or that of the influence of the sculptures in Cluny III, the aggregate influence of Cluny in both spheres was very great.

(Of course, the analogy drawn above (p. 22) between Cluny and feudalism must not be pressed. The theses[15] that Cluny propagated feudalism, or supported pilgrimages to pacify the masses are unhistorical.)

Notes

1   The following are some recent studies on Cluny: K. J. Conant, *Cluny, Les Eglises et la Maison du chef d'Ordre* (Mâcon, 1968). G. Constable, *The Letters of Peter the Venerable*, 2 vols (Cambridge, Mass., 1967). id., and J. Kritzeck, 'Petrus Venerabilis, 1156-1956', *Studia Anselmiana* 40 (Rome, 1957). H. E. J. Cowdrey, *The Cluniacs and the Gregorian Reform* (Oxford, 1970). G. Duby, *La Société aux xi et xii siècles dans la région mâconnaise* (Paris, 1957). K. Hallinger, 'Gorze-Kluny', *Studia Anselmiana* 22-25 (Rome, 1950). N. Hunt, *Cluny under St Hugh* (London, 1967); id. (edit.), *Cluniac Monasticism in the Central Middle Ages* (London, 1971); G. Tellenbach, *Neue Forschungen über Cluny und die Cluniacenser* (Freiburg, 1959).

2   *Annales O.S.B.* VI 518-9 (Lucca, 1745).

3   A. Bruel, *Recueil des chartes de l'abbaye de Cluny* (Paris, 6 vols, 1876-1903), p. 112.

4   Gregory's allocution is printed in full by Cowdrey (*op. cit.*, note 1), pp. 272-3.

5   See M. D. Knowles, 'The Reforming Decrees of Peter the Venerable', in Constable, *Petrus Venerabilis* (note 1).

6   Ulrich, *Consuetudines Cluniacenses*, Migne, Pat. Lat. cxlix coll. 668,688. Cf. also the anonymous *Life of Hugh*, Pat. Lat. clix. coll. 925-6.

7   K. Hallinger, 'Le climat spirituel des premiers temps de Cluny', *Revue Mabillon* 46 (1956), pp. 117-140. English trans. in Hunt (note 1), pp. 191 ff. J. Leclercq, 'La crise au monachisme aux xi et xii siècles'. *Bulletino dell'instituto Storico Italiano per il medio evo*, No. 70 (Rome, 1958). English trans. in Hunt, *Monasticism* (note 1), pp. 217 ff.

8   See *Eremitismo in Occidente nei secoli xi e xii* (Milan, 1965). Report of Study Week at Mendola 1962 in *Publications of the University of the Sacred Heart*.

9   Bernard, Letter 1 in all edd. Migne Pat. Lat. clxxxii coll. 67 ff.

10   Constable, *Letters of Peter the Venerable* (note 1 above) II, pp. 293-5, lists six Cluniac cardinals between 1122 and 1156, and between 1132 and 1164 six important non-Cluniac English houses received Cluniac abbots. Cf. Knowles, *Monastic Order in England* (Cambridge, 1940), pp. 283-4.

11   Note 3 above.

12   Gregory VII *Register*, ed. Caspar viii 3, p. 520.

13   E. Delaruelle, 'L'idée de croissade dans la littérature clunisienne', *Annales du Midi* 75 (Toulouse, 1963). English trans. in Hunt (note 1) *Cluniac Monasticism*, pp. 192-216, and Cowdrey (*op. cit.* note 1), pp. 180-7.

14   See Conant (*op. cit.*, note 1) and id., *Carolingian and Romanesque Architecture* (London, 1959), pp. 91-125.

15   E. Werner, *Die gesellschaftlichen Grundlagen des Klosterreform im 11. Jht* (Berlin, 1953). B. Topfer, 'Reliquienkult und Pilgerbewegung zur Zeit der Klosterreform', in H. Sproemberg and H. Kretzschman, *Vom Mittelter zur Neuzeit* (Berlin, 1956), pp. 420-39.

Hans Kramer

Commitment and Fidelity in the Religious Life

FOR a number of years divorce has been a topic of discussion in the Catholic Church and departures from the celibate priesthood have begun to worry parishes. Similarly, the faithful are now beginning to look with doubt and anxiety at the religious commitment required in religious life. Can and should this sort of personal dedication be lifelong? Should a single decision be irrevocable throughout life? Is a commitment of this sort meaningful, humanly possible or even desirable?[1]

COUNSELS

One possible way of understanding the total religious commitment demanded by the evangelical counsels is offered by the various modern views of man which see him as the intersection of various forms of existence. Three lines intersect in man, natural development, socio-cultural formation and the individual's forming of himself. There is no need to be a specialist in human anthropology to know that these different lines do not just produce a convergence, but also inevitable divergences which may threaten existence; this is a matter of general experience. It means that no human being can escape the call to an ascetism which must be affirmative, constructive, negative and reductive. A Christian who commits himself to the religious life undertakes this asceticism in a special way.

1. Discovery of Psycho-Social Identity

It is clear that in addition to this, for the person who is suited to it and equipped for it, the commitment of his whole life to the following of the counsels is a particularly suitable way of discovering personal and cultural identity (group identity). Today we are in advance of classical psychoanalysis in being aware that this involves a formative process not only in the nucleus of the individual but also within the culture of the community, in social role expectations and obligations.[2]

Subjectively, this identity, which is both something achieved and something to be constantly re-achieved, takes the form of a reinforcing sense of personal stability and continuity, which does not, however, exclude changes. A healthy group identity or cultural identity can be measured by the number of personal and social interactions, the degree of capacity and willingness for dialogue and the extent to which these capacities are put to use.

The psycho-social potential for discovering their identities is made available to the religious when their orders are fully aware of their commitment to the New Testament message and the main intentions of their founders. This presupposes that the postulant has acquired, in childhood and adolescence, basic confidence, independence, initiative and the ability to act and take decisions. In this process religious commitment in the forms of poverty, obedience and chaste celibacy is particularly helpful in creating a healthy self-understanding and sense of selfhood (identity). The choice of a group for oneself with particular leaders and models brings about a new appraisal and affirmation of one's identity. The ego of the religious man or woman is relocated within the immediate and the wider community. What distinguishes this from the process of joining other groups is that it is guided by humane and religious values.

The signposts of the religious life also draw attention to dangers, as when ideological interpretations creep in to justify obedience, mortification or mission, but it nevertheless remains true that this pattern of life can claim to offer psychological health.

2. Stimulated Awareness

Commitment to the religious life confers no fixed status. A religious undertakes a particular form of voluntary exposure. He declares himself open, and people make demands on him. Demands which take his willingness for granted produce a higher degree of awareness in a life consciously conducted; the religious constantly re-exposes himself to the needs and the standard of others.

The special situation of following Christ and the ideal standards of the community of disciples give rise to other disturbing reflections: he must ask whether he is living up to the word, spirit and actions of Christ and the Church.

II.   RELIGIOUS SIGNIFICANCE OF RELIGIOUS LIFE

Particularly inspiring and illuminating for our time are attempts to see Jesus' group of disciples as a model of commitment to the evangelical counsels in the Church.[3]

1. Listening and Learning

Jesus' disciples are an exemplary sign for Christian religious as group of pupils who really followed him and lived with him. The aspects of service and shared suffering in particular have to be understood by listening to the word of Jesus and learning from his fate. Of course all Christians have the duty of listening to the word of Jesus and learning from him, 'but commitment to the counsels emphasises by a symbolic life which is an example for the whole Church how important and necessary it is for everyone to listen to the message of Jesus and learn from him.'[4]

2. Collaboration

Jesus called his disciples and sent them out as his fellow workers. Their demonstrative adherence to him and public listening to him was not enough on its own. The existence of the group of disciples is indeed in itself a promise and exhortation, but testimony in word and action is required as well. Like their master, the disciples have to proclaim the arrival of the power of God in this world and bring it about by a pastoral struggle against the power of evil (Lk. 11.20; Mk; 3.15) and by their authority to heal (Lk. 7.18-23; Lk. 10.9). In this sense the pastoral ministry, the care of the sick, the preaching of the word and other particular tasks of a religious group are a charismatic witness to God and to the coming of his kingdom.

Commitment to the counsels takes its basic structure from the disciples of Jesus: men and women try, according to their inclination and spiritual gifts, to be sign for the Church and the world in their whole existence in listening and service. They show in a special way what is necessary for all.

3. A Vow as an Answer to the Lord's Counsels

'Although the "three counsels" of the Church's tradition may not yet have been explicitly formulated as three, they were nevertheless required in practice and lived among the disciples of Jesus.'[5]

This becomes particularly clear in what H. Schurmann singles out as counsels addressed to the disciples. Their original context is the teaching directed to the disciples, but in the post-Easter community they retained their meaning, now transformed by Easter, and were for that reason handed on. Submission is urged at a deeper level, particularly in the aspect of perseverance (Mk. 10.38). As an extension of doing without a home, renunciation of marriage is recommended 'for the sake of the kingdom of heaven' (Mt. 19.11-12). As an extension of the abandonment of possessions there is a demand for a total serenity which relies on God alone (Lk. 12.33-34; Lk. 10.4; Mk. 6.7ff).

These appeals and counsels claim the whole life of the person addressed, not only in its depth but also throughout its length. Here the purpose and course of Jesus' life is in itself the most forceful 'counsel'. Looking back from the plough is no longer possible (Lk. 9.62). In this way the counsels become the almost necessary and natural requirement for life in the emphatic-demonstrative symbolic mode of the counsels. They are a response to the God who calls and inspires us in Christ. They give a direction to the freedom of the individual Christian who takes up his responsibility. They also mark the beginning of authoritative activity for the Church and the world which are their objects.[6]

III.   WHY IRREVOCABLE FIDELITY?

Even the Vatican Council and its attempt to rethink and reshape religious life has not succeeded in making the Christian and ecclesial quality of religious orders stand out in local churches with greater sharpness. This is shown by the diminishing number of applicants, particularly in Europe. A particularly important factor in this, however, seems to be that in the older moral tradition of the Church insufficient attention was given to the virtue of fidelity.

1. Fidelity, the Forgotten Virtue

A common view, which follows Thomas Aquinas, regards fidelity as a virtue subordinate to justice and parallel to honesty. On this view fidelity is the willingness to make actions match promises. It is seen predominantly as a contractual relationship. In such a heavily legalistic approach it is almost inevitable that the relevant discussions should be very interested in determining when this contractual relationship is no longer binding. But fidelity can and must be looked at in a much more complex way, and if it is so looked at it turns out to be a fundamental Christian virtue. In this light it must be regarded as the foundation of irrevocable decisions made by Christians, as truth to oneself, as direct truth or fidelity to another — man or God — and indirect fidelity to another.

Every form of fidelity includes an element of truth to oneself. Defining oneself is the future in the affirmation of the past. In making a promise a person puts down a permanent pledge in the face of all changes in his inner feelings or in external circumstances. In addition to this fidelity as fidelity to another is an interpersonal relation. It links

I and Thou and I and We, and so shows itself to be an aspect of love as well as of justice. Love means existing and acting for the benefit of others. Fidelity gives love its effectiveness. Its role is to persevere through sacrifice and renunciation. Fidelity leads us to make commitments to persons and values which are intended to be irrevocable. Fidelity is a matter of the 'heart' (Mt. 22.37; Rom. 10.10), not the intellect, will or emotions alone. Fidelity to the good, which is confirmed and made public in promises, prevents the fragmentation of the ego and encourages the coordination of the forces of the personality.

2. Human Fidelity

A Christian is prepared for new ethical reflections on the subject of fidelity because both the Old and New Testaments present God as the faithful God who in both the Old and New Covenants preserves an unbreakable relationship with his people. In return God requires man to keep faith as his covenant partner, by observing the principles of the covenant in his life, being faithful to God and keeping faith with his fellow men.

God shows himself to be faithful in both rewarding and punishing (Mt. 10.18; 18.1-11, etc; Lk. 15.11-32). Christ is the supreme proof of God's fidelity (Rev. 1.5; Acts 2-3). He demands an answering fidelity of men, in trust and hope, steadfastness and obedience, patience, long-suffering, expectancy and endurance. The call for faithfulness is most explicit in the call to discipleship, and secondly in the exhortations to confident hope and faithful patience as fundamental attitudes in the Christian life. Christian life as a whole is dominated by the demand for fidelity as obedience.[7]

IV.   HELP IN MAKING LIFE COMMITMENTS

The drastic character of the fidelity required by morality and Christian revelation is expressed in commitments which are declared in the Church to be irrevocable: in faith, in marriage, in promises and oaths, in vows. This gives rise, however, to the urgent question of how a person can reach sufficient personal maturity to make a commitment of himself and his actions binding in faith for the whole of his future life.

1. Preparation for Vows

A remark by the Vatican Council about the conditions necessary for the making of vows has attracted particular attention and approval. In connexion with the vow of celibate chastity the Council said that the candidates should not 'be admitted to the profession except after a truly adequate testing period and only if they have the needed degree of psychological and emotional maturity'.[8]

This maturity involves three main requirements. Their formulation reveals the need for educational and psychological concepts which are on the whole new to Christian education. In particular, the individual's perception, sense of values and capacity for value judgements must be stimulated, nourished and developed.

First, in childhood and adolescence he must become capable of a confident perception of reality. Perception is learnt through an enquiring encounter with objects, and in this process the passive and active imagination (phantasy) should be particularly fostered as a personal instrument for the discovery of reality. Next, the sense of values should be fostered as a preliminary stage to moral decisions. The principal element in this is emotional development, the most important contributions to which are those of the parents and educators of the young. Thirdly, choosing of values, personal decisions on what is morally valid, must be learnt and practised. The individual must be brought to a freedom and autonomy in which he can establish feelings and attitudes, an orientation, towards himself and his actions, a process which normally takes place in the small and almost invisible preliminaries to decision.[9]

2. Degrees of Maturity Required for Religious Commitment

The maturity required for the making of a vow can be broken down into a number of separate components. These differ with the approaches of different philosophical and psychological theories, but a useful division takes account of three basic desires.[10]

(a)   The Desire for Pleasure and the Celibate Life

A first condition for a lifelong commitment to celibacy is an emotionally mature attitude to one's body and a corresponding use of it.

Sexuality, which pervades every level of the personality and all abilities, must be accepted as good. Not only must one's own sexuality be accepted, but the nature of the other sex must be recognised and respected in its various forms. The polarity between man and woman, which goes far beyond the sexual, must also be recognised.

The vow of celibacy requires a well-developed capacity for unselfish personal love, because it is this which transforms the desire and ambivalence of eros.

(b)   The Desire for Power and the Commitment to Obedience

An openness to dialogue, understood in a general sense, must be present if a believer is to be able to commit himself to lifelong obedience. The self-giving and acceptance of the other which take place in dialogue require a person to have restrained his tendencies to dominate others.

The necessary maturity also includes the ability and willingness to take responsibility for oneself and others. This means knowing one's own capacities and having enough self-confidence to trust others.

A person who wishes to live a life of religious obedience must have his desire for power under such control that he can advance others for their benefit.

(c)   The Desire for Wealth and Acceptance of Poverty

Maturity in the desire for wealth is a state in which material and intellectual goods can be ranked according to their instrumental and intrinsic value and in which appropriate attitudes to them can be developed according to their value.

A person who vows himself to poverty should also be capable of tolerating frustration in the sense of being able to accept the rejection of justified claims without producing a depressive or aggressive reaction.

Lastly the maturity required for poverty in a religious community includes the ability to give and accept gifts.

3. Aids to Fidelity in the Religious Life

The maturity in a person's attitude to life must have been shown in tangible form, though it may be still in its beginnings, when a man or woman commits his or her life to God in a vow intended as irrevocable. If the community of which the Christian becomes a member provides all the psychological and spiritual aids necessary for full human development, the vows become a means of further development and maturing of the personality. They encourage a growth and deepening of the chosen attitude to life. Essential requirements in the common life of religious are collaborative exchange and a willingness to learn from one's brothers and sisters.

One thing which prevents the aspect of communicative fidelity from being seen in vows is the definition of a vow in Canon 1307 as a promise made to God with regard to some good. Since the second Vatican Council this definition has become superfluous, since it gives too much emphasis to the transfer of some object. In fact the important thing is not the gift which is promised. The gift is a symbol of self-giving and self-dedication. In the gift the giver offers himself. This view makes clearer the relation of a vow to the baptismal vow, which is the Christian's fundamental act of surrender.[11] It also makes it clearer that what is involved is basically an attitude of personal fidelity. This clarification is extremely important.

V. RENUNCIATION OF COMMITMENT

These and other criteria of maturity have been firmly established by the modern study of personality, and without them no irrevocable commitment to a life according to the evangelical counsels is possible. It follows from this that many people who have made vows which formally and from the point of view of canon law were valid were not psychologically (and therefore morally) capable of doing so. As the theological principle states, grace builds on nature.

For moral theology, no irrevocable vow exists in these cases. The best thing for such religious, for several reasons, would seem to be, if possible and perhaps with specialist help, to create a human foundation for their religious life. This imposes on the Church and orders an urgent obligation to take responsibility for providing professionally qualified help in their own institutions. Where this is not provided, or where the religious concerned are unwilling to attempt this extremely difficult process, which may in some circumstances involve individual or group therapy, canon law and public opinion in the Church must give them the opportunity of leaving the religious life without additional hardships and without damage to their dignity or reputation.

1. Renunciation for Reasons of Fidelity of Commitments intended as Irrevocable

Fidelity is the aspect of love which involves renunciation, sacrifice, steadfastness and sometimes suffering. As such, it is a morally valuable attitude which should be part of every life. Fidelity seeks expression in promises or vows, which means, in dialogue. To break such promises arbitrarily or without sufficient reason contradicts fidelity.

There are, however, degrees of fidelity, more peripheral and more central forms. From this it follows that the less central form must give way before a higher fidelity, although the form first chosen must be 'transcended' in the higher form; it cannot be simply negatively abrogated, but must be in some way included in the higher form. The comradeship of childhood, for example, is not just negatively abandoned. It was appropriate to one stage, and later it becomes part of the friendships of adolescence, which have a different structure. The fidelity involded in these friendships also has an end, but its quality goes over into the later fidelity of married love.

These are degrees of fidelity according to maturity, but there are also degrees according to the object. Such a case is when fidelity to a single person conflicts with fidelity to many. There are also degrees according to the status of the obligation, private or public, legal or extra-legal, secular or religious, etc. Fidelity as such is irrevocable. It is an obligation on everyone. Fidelity can only be instantiated in particular forms of life, but a person may be morally justified in retracting a commitment to such a particular form if this enables him to practise his fidelity in more appropriate forms.

A mature decision to enter the religious life involves so many dimensions – personal, social, religious and ecclesiastical – that in normal circumstances it is as irrevocable as it was intended and as its nature demands.

However, there are certain conditions implied by such a commitment on the part of the mature believer. The religious takes up a position towards a particular community and its ideals, he envisages a particular Church with a particular structure, he expects his life to take definite directions. This may give rise to defects as a result of which it is morally permissible to go back on a promise or vow made with the intention that it should be irrevocable. When there is really nothing the person concerned can do about the defects, to renounce the vow becomes a duty. In these circumstances a public settlement with the community is very much in the interest of the religious concerned. In this still imperfect world it is wrong for canon law to start from the assumption that the defects are always on the side of the individual. The law of the Church is the law of a community, but in its concern for the welfare of the community it should not attack the integrity of someone who opposes community structures and practices on conscientious grounds. The formal settlement procedures, their staff, duration and methods, should be such as to allow mistakes made by orders and others to be recognised, publicly admitted and abandoned in the spirit of Christian brotherly correction. It should be obvious that respect for conscience and dignity, and discretion in general, need to be observed on all sides.

2. Renunciation involving a Breach of Faith

There can also be a renunciation of vows originally intended as irrevocable which involves a breach of faith. In this case the members of the Church must resist the temptation to interfere in the individual's conscience; their concern can go no further than the preservation of order in the Church. This follows from the nature of law as such, but the obligation is strengthened by the voluntary nature of Christian morality, which must totally reject any compulsion on personal moral decisions. In such matters canon law must fix limits of toleration and defend the freedom of conscience even of those who are not in good faith.

3. Some Remarks on Ecclesiastical Dispensations from Vows

The prevailing doctrine explains the Church's action of dispensing from vows in terms of a theory of 'remission'. The making of a vow is regarded as establishing a contractual relationship or a relationship of obligation between God and the person making the vow. But, runs the argument, God can always waive the exercise of his rights over the other party, and Christ has given his Church authority to remit obligations arising out of vows. Thus when the Church dispenses someone from a vow it is as though God declared that from now on he was releasing that person from the obligation to fulfil his promise.[12]

There are many unanswerable objections to this view. One of the most important is based on a theory of the 'determination of facts'. In terms of this view it has been shown that a dispensation is not really a remission of obligations arising from the vow but a declaration embodying a judgment that as a matter of fact the obligation arising out of the vow has ceased to exist. The legal position is not altered, but clarified.[13] An analysis of the grounds required by the existing legal procedure for dispensation from vows shows that in all cases the moral basis for the performance of the vow has disappeared. For reasons deriving either from his personality or from the situation, the person who made the vow is incapable of performing the relevant obligations.[14]

Attention to this point should contribute to making the legal procedure simpler and more correct. It will enable the existence of vows in the Church to be recognised once more as primarily a matter of morality, and give new prominence to fidelity as the basis for vows of religion as a response to the faithful God.

Translated by Francis McDonagh

Notes

1   For recent studies of these problems cf. H. Kramer, *Unwiderrufliche Entscheidungen im Leben des Christen* (Paderborn, 1974); K. Demmer, *Die Lebensentscheidung* (Paderborn, 1974).

2   Particularly stimulating discussions of the psychological and sociological aspects are contained in two books by E. H. Erikson, *Identity and the Life Cycle* (New York, 1959); *Identity, Youth and Crisis* (New York, 1968).

3   H. Schürmann, 'Der Jüngerkreis Jesu als Zeichen für Israel', *Ursprung und Gesalt. Erörterungnen und Besinnungen zum Neuen Testament* (Düsseldorf, 1970), pp. 45-60.

4   Schürmann, 'Der Jüngerkreis Jesu', p. 49.

5   Schürmann, p. 54.

6   It is still necessary to stress that this does not mean an advocacy of a double standard. Making a vow and joining an order are ways of carrying out an obligation laid on all Christians. The difference is one of symbolic status, which always depends on a gift and call from God.

7   K. H. Schelke, *Theologie des Neuen Testaments*, vol. 3: *Ethos*, (Düsseldorf, 1970), pp. 39-40.

8   Vatican II, *Decree on the Appropriate Renewal of the Religious Life*, 12; *Instruction on the Appropriate Renewal of the Religious Life*, 4.

9   In psychological terms there is no such thing as a 'basic decision' in the sense of a beginning or initial discussion. The hypothesis of 'non-decision', which might have been relevant to this topic, has not been adequately supported and must be regarded as disproved.

10   On what follows cf. especially J. Köhne, 'Gedanken zur Noviziatsgestaltung aus ärztlicher Sicht', in Vereinigung deutscher Ordensobern, *Noviziätsgestaltung Heute. Werkwoche der Novizenmeister 1968* (Cologne, 1968), pp. 17-30.

11   Vatican II, *Decree on Religious Life*, 12; *Constitution on the Church*, 44.

12   H. Kramer, *Unwiderrufliche Entscheidungnen*, pp. 236-48, 273-85.

13 J. Lederer, 'Der Dispensbegriff des kanonischen Rechts unter besonderer Berüksichtigung der Rechtssprache des CIC', *Münchener Theol. Studien, Kanonische Abteilung* 8 (1957), pp. 98-106.

14 R. Ginters, 'Versprechen und Geloben. Begründens-weisen ihrer sittlichen Verbindlichkeit', *Moraltheol. Studien, Systematische Abteilung* 1 (Düsseldorf, 1973), pp. 177-9.

Aquinata Böckmann

Evangelical Poverty, the Welfare State, and the Third World

TWO assumptions may be produced in the mind of the unprejudiced reader by the sight of this title in this context. He may imagine, first, that evangelical poverty has something to do with the future of religious life, and second, that there is a discrepancy on the one hand between what is practised in religious life as 'evangelical poverty' and what this means in scripture and on the other between religious 'poverty' and social poverty. This article deals primarily with evangelical poverty rather than social poverty, but the second cannot be ignored since it is reasonable to assume that a life of religious poverty cannot be lived without some relation to social poverty. The main importance of evangelical poverty is its meaning, not its forms or practical implementation. It has a meaning; it points to something. It is not an ideal in itself, but is in the service of something greater. But we must then ask for whom it is meant to have a meaning or stand for something, and this again implies that the actual situation cannot be ignored.

The Vatican II Decree on Religious Life lays down two criteria for poverty, imitation of Christ and sharing in his poverty and adaptation to the changed conditions of the time.[1] The following section will show briefly that neither of these was very important in the traditional interpretation of 'evangelical poverty'.

I. RELIGIOUS POVERTY IN THE RESTRICTED JURIDICAL SENSE

It is a striking feature of many older ascetic books written for religious that they do not discuss the vow of poverty in relation to Jesus Christ or the Gospel. If they appear at all, biblical quotations are decorative trimmings; they can be removed without detriment to the structure of the argument. The real basis of the presentation is canon law and its concept of religious poverty as the surrender of the right of possession or free use of material goods. It is typical in this context that van Acken should answer the question why a person who has unnecessary or over-expensive possessions has offended against poverty, not by a reference to the poverty of Christ or his radical demands, but with the reason that 'canon law expressly lays down that all the household goods of religious must be suitable to the poverty they have embraced (Can. 594 part 3 . . . 2). Because those who live in the world would rightly take scandal . . .'[2] Because renunciation of the free exercise of the right of ownership is regarded as the substance of the simple vow, the main point of interest is requests for permissions, and the essence of poverty shifts to dependence on superiors in the use of material goods. For many treatises the other main element is thrift. One author advises: 'Do not be too fond of giving presents, even with permission. You are poor. You are supposed to have nothing and can therefore give nothing.'[3] Thus a literal minded attitude can make it more difficult to approach the socially poor.

The meaning of this poverty is regarded mainly as being that it removes obstacles to perfection, promotes interior detachment and stimulates acts of virtue. It is 'the rampart of the spiritual life and of the whole discipline of religion'.[4] This attitude could still be seen in the first draft of the Decree on the Religious life, which said (part 78) that the religious is purified by poverty of worldly desires and made a stranger to earhtly things. It is also remarked that individual poverty contributes to the economic balance of the monastery.

The title and subtitle of this article in themselves indicate a movement away from this restricted juridical view. It is noteworthy that the first question discussed in an issue devoted to canon law should not be a legal one but the meaning of evangelical poverty and its point in modern situations.

II. EVANGELICAL POVERTY IN THE NEW TESTAMENT?

1. The Poverty of Jesus Christ

2 Cor. 8.9: 'Though he was rich, yet for your sake he became poor, so that by his poverty you might become rich.' In the hymn in Philippians (Phil. 2.6-11) this becoming poor is described in terms of 'self-annihilation' (*kenosis*) and humiliation. The incarnation and dispossession to the point of death on the cross are the ontological basis of the poverty of Jesus. Poverty is an essential aspect of the mystery of Christ and the redemption, and is not just a renunciation of material goods or of their use, but goes further to a renunciation of divine privi-

leges, of ruling and power. It is a self-dispossession, 'making oneself like men', not for the sake of poverty but for love of men. Evangelical poverty is not an end in itself, but an expression of love and an instrument of service. The Son of man comes to serve and to give his life as a ransom for many (cf. Mk. 10.45 par.). In its various forms Christ's becoming poor is to save the poor. Poverty in itself is not an ideal; it is to be overcome, but – and this is the fundamental paradox of poverty – by being accepted. In the incarnation Jesus becomes the brother of all of us. He becomes a member of an unimportant people, in which he does not belong to the ruling class, and lives in a despised village. It is not the striking poverty of a beggar, but a sharing in the destiny of ordinary people, immersion in the greyness of everyday life, inconspicuousness and finally solidarity with the pain of a life which ends in failure and death.

This existential solidarity appears in Jesus' public life in the conscious approach to the little people, the unimportant, children, the poor, to all who are in need. The 'Hail to you poor!', as the original version of Lk. 6.20 has it, is programmatic. No questions are asked about the merits or attitudes of the poor; it is because they are needy that they are the privileged class of the kingdom of God. God's love is such that it goes out to the humblest, and in Jesus Christ this love appeared. The God of the poor, the Messiah, appeared. His coming is the coming of the messianic age of happiness (cf. Is. 61.1; Mt. 11.5 pars.). The arrival of the herald of this mighty kingdom of God produces a reversal of values (cf. Lk. 1.46-55; 6.20-26).

Jesus demonstrates his affection for the poor not just by making approaches to them (from an inaccessible height, as we might imagine it), but by himself descending into utter poverty. Because he is poor himself he can invite all those who labour and are burdened to come to him (Mt. 11.28-29). He is the model of the poor man as described in the Old Testament spirituality of poverty, poor to the depths of his heart, humble before God, bowing before him, patient and trusting, open to his will, constantly giving way before him (cf. the gospel of John). This rootedness of his poverty in something else enables him to overcome any fanaticism of poverty which would look for heroic deprivations for their own sake. Jesus displays an inner calm in relation to the various actual forms poverty takes. What is more important is that it serves the mission. Nor does solidarity with the poor turn into class fanaticism; he is available to all who need him, even the rich.

2. The Poverty of the Disciples

Jesus calls people to follow him. Of individuals he makes a radical demand for the renunciation of all their possessions, and of all disciples availability for his mission and a sharing of his fate. He gives frequent warnings about the dangers of wealth (especially in Luke), and refers to a choice between God and Mammon (Mt. 6.25; Lk. 16.13). In the evangelists' editing we can see a transfer of the conditions for discipleship to all Christians. Matthew develops the triumphant cry 'Hail to you poor!' into a sort of catechism for the community of disciples in which he describes the conditions for being a follower of the Messiah: poverty in spirit (to the depths of the heart), gentleness, hunger and thirst for righteousness, compassion, purity of heart, steadfastness under persecution (Mt. 5.3-10). This does not mean a denial of real poverty; it is accepted, deepened in an attitude of poverty before God, made practical in a turning towards the needy and involves all areas of life.

The poverty of the disciples is related to the poor of the period. Renunciation of possessions and a simple life make it possible to give alms (cf. Mk. 10.21; Lk. 12.33). The disciples are told to welcome the poor into their table fellowship (Lk. 14.12-14, 21), to receive children (Mk. 9.37) and, like Jesus himself, proclaim the good news to the poor (cf. Mt. 10.6ff). They have a common purse, and are told to form a brotherhood without competing for places of honour (Mt. 23.8; Mk. 9.35), in mutual service, following the example of Christ (Lk. 22.24-27). Luke develops this idea in Acts, where he describes the primitive Christian community as a brotherhood, communion (2.42-47; 4.32-35). In the tradition of the Old Testament spirituality of poverty, he explains that they shared their possessions so that there were no poor among them. For Hellenistic readers he describes the communion as a friendly society in which all things were common. The sharing of the eucharistic bread, the community around the exalted Lord, spreads into a sharing or shared use of material goods. In 1 Cor. 11.17-34, Paul shows that sharing in the Lord's Supper necessarily requires an equalising of possessions among Christians. On a different level he organises the collection for Jerusalem, the point of which is not to make the others materially poor (2 Cor. 8.13-14) but to enable them to share in the continuation of Christ's act of love and thus to establish a communion going beyond the local community (2 Cor. 8.8-9.24).

Poverty as a fundamental attitude in the life of the disciple has its root in an attitude of poverty before God. The disciples are forced to recognise their complete helplessness; they all abandon Jesus, and Peter betrays him. Mk. 10.23-27 makes clear that it is extremely difficult, not just for the rich, but for anyone and for the disciples as well, to enter the kingdom of God, that it is in fact impossible. Neither possessions nor renunciation of possessions (however heroic) can achieve it; it is a gift. Human beings are powerless to save themselves, but God's marvellous power can intervene for everyone and make all things possible (Mk. 10.27). The radical poverty of man before God is contrasted with any speculation on merit or reward! Whatever he may do, the disciple is still an unprofitable servant (Lk. 17.10). Paul describes himself as a 'slave of Christ', and lives in the belief that God's power reaches its full scope in his weakness (2 Cor. 12.9-10; cf. 1 Cor. 15.10). From the knowledge of this powerlessness before God Jesus leads the disciples on to trust in dependence on the Father who looks after everything (Mt. 6.25-34 pars.). They will be Jesus' messengers and in this poverty will preach, not themselves and their own teaching, but Jesus Christ and his cross (Lk. 10.16; 2 Cor. 4.5; 1 Cor. 2.1-5).

But this attitude of total poverty before God must take specific forms. Certainly the disciples who follow Jesus cannot weigh themselves down with luggage. In the missionary speeches extreme frugality is demanded: they are told to be satisfied with what is offered to them in the houses they visit (Mk. 6.10). For Paul, being a 'slave of Christ', poverty before God takes the form of earning his living with his own hands, even though he knows the saying of the Lord that the labourer is worthy of his hire (cf. 1 Cor. 9.14). The rooting of poverty in a larger aim nevertheless makes the external forms relative. Paul is familiar with poverty and hunger, as he is with their opposite (Phil. 4.11-12). The New Testament shows a special affection for the poor, but this never takes on the tone of the class struggle. The distinctions between rich and poor, masters and slaves, are swept away by faith: all are one and equal in Christ (Gal. 3.28; cf. Jas. 1.9-10). From this the practical conclusion is drawn that respect for persons should have no place in the community of Christ. Christ's message carries within it the power to transform structures from within.

3. The Meaning of Evangelical Poverty

There is no one thing in the New Testament which is evangelical poverty. It is more like a general term describing a basic attitude of discipleship which takes a variety of particular forms. Important elements include renunciation of wealth, but even more important are serenity, freedom to serve, help for the poor and sharing – based on an attitude of poverty before God. The Gospel contains no rigid law of poverty, no single set of rules for all, but wide variability, even contradictoriness in the various forms. What is important is the intention of Jesus, the meaning, which is preserved through the changes of form.

The rich man's renunciation of his wealth, the guarantee of God's blessing and of participation in the final salvation, is a sign of the novelty and incomparable greatness of the kingdom of God which is dawning in the person of Jesus (cf. also Mt. 13.44-46). All salvation and all security is now to be found in him. In the original version of the missionary discourses (Q, represented in Mt. 10.9-10) purses, bags, money, even sandals and staff are forbidden – an almost impossible demand, to be understood only in the light of the prophetic tradition of symbolic actions. In itself, this extreme poverty is pointless, but it points towards the greatness of the kingdom of God which towers over all earthly values. No human resources can express it. Paul describes a similar paradox in his references to 'the folly of the cross' and 'power in weakness' (cf. 1 Cor. 1.18-31).

The essence of the kingdom of God is that it turns our human standards upside down. The rich God becomes a poor child; he associates mainly with the poor. He who is the ruler becomes the servant of all. When the disciples quarrel about who is the greatest he shows them a child (Mk. 9.36). Human values such as power, wealth, honour, and so on, fade before the splendour of this kingdom; our works (including our renunciations) cannot merit it — it can only be a gift (cf. Mk. 10. 12-16). This extremism in poverty is a symbol not only of the greatness of the kingdom of God but also of God's love, which became visible in Jesus. We cannot fully grasp the paradox of poverty intellectually. Jesus' warnings against wealth emphasise one reason: riches bring with them the danger that people may look for security in them and finally lose their openness to transcendence and their sense of their radical indigence. And on the other hand deprivation and poverty may keep alive in man an awareness of the need to depend on God for fulfilment.

A second meaning of the renunciation of possessions is illustrated by the call of the rich young man. The main point is not that he should free himself inwardly from the ties of wealth, but giving it away is a precondition of discipleship (Mk. 10.21). Voluntary poverty means freedom to share one's life with Jesus and thereby share in his mission. Mark's version of the missionary address in particular stresses this point. The editor expressly allows, correcting his original, staff and sandals (Mk. 6.8-9). He wants to see the message spread quickly. (The staff may be seen as a sign of readiness to keep on the move.) Whatever encourages this is allowed. For the period of persecution, Lk. 22.36 provides that the disciples may equip themselves for their missionary journeys with a purse, money and a sword. But what comes across in all the versions of the missionary discourse is that poverty makes the messengers credible. Similarly for Paul, his particular form of poverty, earning his living by manual work, is intended to add credibility to his preaching. Jesus himself gives up privacy and a permanent home for the sake of his mission.

There is yet another strand of meaning in the New Testament. Wealth leads us to ignore the poorer brethren (Lk. 16.20-21). The rich young man's renunciation of his possessions is to be for the benefit of the poor (Mk. 10.21 pars.). The poverty of the individual members of the first community is a precondition for brotherhood, makes possible a communion around the exalted Lord going beyond the local community (Paul's collection). And at the same time this community of goods points to the coming kingdom of God in which all, rich and poor, will share in the final salvation; it stands for the love which is willing to share, in imitation of the love of Christ, who dispossessed himself for us. In this way it demonstrates that we belong to the Messiah, and by allowing us to share his poverty can contribute to salvation and redemption.

III. THE RELIGIOUS AIM OF EVANGELICAL POVERTY

In spite of the widespread opinion that there is no sense in making a vow of poverty because poverty is not a value, it is by now quite clear that what evangelical poverty stands for (ignoring the idealisation of material poverty) is still a valid and worthwhile aim.

From the Gospel we have seen that renunciation of 'possessions' can no longer be defined simply in terms of a renunciation of material values because the form of possession has changed sharply in the course of time. The resources of religious communities and individuals today are not so much articles of luxury as productive power, which serves the poor best not by gift-giving but by being put to socially useful work. Skills, knowledge, training and labour power are much more valuable forms of possession than material resources. This (and not only the Gospel) means that religious poverty must to a much greater extent involve renunciation of the use of these goods for private profit, in other words being at the service of others with one's possessions and one's self, which again requires dispossession.

Evangelical poverty as attempted by religious orders may perhaps be defined as the imitation of Christ in the sharing of goods and the service of and solidarity with the poor. Of course, it must be remembered throughout that, in conformity with the law of the incarnation, all this is only possible in specific practical forms.

1. The Meaning of Religious Poverty in a Welfare State

The first strand of meaning in evangelical poverty, its pointing to the greatness and uniqueness of the kingdom of God, is beyond the range of secular standards and for that reason seems to be particularly important in our saturated environment as a form of social criticism. In the face of a trend to constantly higher consumption religious can, by their simplicity, restraint in consumption, lack of collective greed and unconcern with their own advantage in practical activity, awaken a feeling for the right scale of values. They can keep alive an awareness of the primacy of the spiritual. If, for example, their first concern in any undertaking is not profitability, they will remind people that personal and spiritual values are more important than material ones. In a society which increasingly judges things by their usefulness and performance, the poverty of religious can enable them to perform a 'critical ministry' by not treating those they help as objects for their assistance, the unimportant, those who have had a raw deal, who have fallen out of the race, whose lives are not 'worth living'. These above all they must recognise and value as human beings with their own dignity, as brothers in Christ, and they must judge all those they come into contact with, not by their status, reputation, income or usefulness, but for themselves, and receive them accordingly. This applies particularly to behaviour within the community. By acting in this way religious can be a sign of the reversal of standards and of love as the law of the kingdom of God. This understanding of poverty would also mean that they did not try to justify their existence by their social or cultural achievements and let themselves be caught up in a superficial utilitarianism.[5] Particularly the direct apostolate or work among the poor cannot be judged by external achievement.

In a situation in which work and technology often seem to be a threat to real humanity, religious, by a simple life in contentment and happiness, by their use of goods with inner freedom and by willing work, performed without activism, can show that this can be a way to humanise work and technology, and that renunciation need not constrict the personality but is necessary to maturity. It is the eschatological dimension which makes possible true secularity and pleasure in material goods. We only begin to possess things really when we stop grabbing them and keeping them for ourselves (cf. 2 Cor. 6.10; *Gaudium et Spes* 37). Forms of spiritual poverty which are open to and looking towards the future, which accept today's existential uncertainty and bravely lay themselves open to questioning in the confidence that the Lord is accompanying us on our pilgrimage, these keep alive eschatological hope and are a sign of the expectation of final fulfilment. On the other hand material and spiritual wealth lead to immobility; we are diverted into making ourselves comfortable and defending the position we have reached. A life-style which has become bourgeois, a religious life which has declined into a superficial *aggiornamento* and is totally integrated into the values of society no longer raises any question and cannot exercise a criticial function.

The second meaning of evangelical poverty as freedom for service in discipleship (apostolic work or work particularly with the various types of poor) has already been emphasised in many publications. More importantly, individual and collective poverty enable us to develop an understanding of the feelings of the poor of every sort, make action on behalf of the underprivileged credible and release energy and capital for assistance. International orders can prevent rich countries from shutting themselves off in a comfortable ghetto by constant reminders of the Third World. Collective poverty which takes the form of altruistic economic activity with an awareness of world responsibility, can, if carefully adapted with the advices of experts to the present economic situation, make a valuable contribution to economic aid and be an incentive to the creation of a juster world economy.

By their poverty in the form of community of goods, religious can bear witness to the way in which openness to others, sharing of material and spiritual goods, make possible an evangelical brotherhood. They can show how problems such as the relationship of young and old can be solved in the spirit of poverty, by listening to each other, mutual respect and exchange. Evangelical poverty enables them to be living models of communities centred on Jesus Christ.

2. The Meaning of Religious Poverty in the Third World

Here religious poverty as it is lived in practice is generally not poverty by the standards of the environment, even if the religious accept considerable restrictions on the standards of Western countries. For the people of the country entry into the order generally means a rise in social status. This makes it harder to present poverty as a witness to the greatness of the kingdom of God as compared with human values. Religious who make themselves as poor as the poor of the country and want to live among them are often regarded with incomprehension by these poor, whose ambition is to escape from their poverty. Nor can voluntary poverty ever completely reach the same level as the real poverty of the poor. A simple life and manner, a preference for 'poor instruments', a rejection of triumphalism and domination, humility in attention to local forces, reticence and the ability to relinquish task, but especially favouring the poor and needy and proclaiming the Good News to the poor without reward, these are some forms of evangelical poverty which can be a witness to the greatness and gratuitous character of the kingdom of God and to its reversal of values.

An even more important meaning of poverty is perhaps its role as a basis for community, for brotherhood across distinctions of race and class, without respect of persons and acknowledging the value and uniqueness of each individual. In this role religious poverty can be a counterweight to class fanaticism and discrimination and so help to improve structures from within.

But here in particular religious poverty will be concerned with overcoming poverty with the help of Christ and not idealizing it. This can be done by finding ways not just of sharing material goods, but more importantly of transmitting training, knowledge and skills. It can be done by social service, in particular by taking part in development projects as partners, which requires a poverty of spirit, an awareness of people and their potential, and is not just help for the poor but a *joint* movement forward. Efforts to liberate people from poverty and oppression can be made fruitful and meaningful by religious poverty if it is rooted in Christ, in eschatological hope, especially the aspect of fraternity and the use of things in the spirit of poverty, which includes social responsibility. But genuine help calls for experience of poverty on the part of the religious. A secure life in comfort creates a barrier, and removes credibility both from the preaching of the Good News to the poor and from exhortations to the rich to practise social justice. In all these ways the witness of poverty has importance for the ministry. We also find the paradox confirmed that religious cannot eliminate poverty without living in poverty themselves, insofar as this does not hinder essential work.

IV. CONCLUSION

I have distinguished three aspects of the meaning of evangelical poverty. It is a sign of the greatness and gratuitous character of the kingdom of God. It is the basis of service in discipleship (particularly the service of the poor). It is also the basis of evangelical brotherhood around the exalted Lord. All three aspects are universally valid, though with differences of emphasis. To embody this meaning the attitude of poverty must take various practical forms, depending on the surroundings, the aims of the particular religious order and personal charisma. This requires great flexibility and energy. The actual forms of poverty must be constantly judged by the Gospel. Evangelical poverty is a 'thorn in the flesh' which prevents us from sitting back and admiring our achievements. Continuity with the great tradition of poverty, and especially with the Gospel, requires us to study the signs of the times to find an appropriate answer, which will give poverty a real meaning, which means ultimately making it a sign of Christ. This implies that it can only acquire its true meaning through this living connexion with Christ. Poverty of this sort is vital to the future of the religious life.

Translated by Francis McDonagh

Notes

1   Cf. the Decree on Religious Life (*Perfectae Caritatis*), part 13: 'today', 'new expressions', 'corporate witness . . . depending on the circumstances of their location'; part 2, and *Evangelica Testificatio*, Nos. 16-24. The present writer has a heavy debt to the publications (and conversation) of the following French writers: Y, Congar, J. M. Tillard, P. R. Régamey, J. Dupont, A. Ancel, R. Voillaume, and among German writers to F. Wulf.

2   Cf. e.g. van Acken, *Lebensschule für Ordensfrauen* (Paderborn, 8th ed. 1953), p. 310.

3   L. Studerus, *Geistliche Lebens- oder Ordensschule für Christen und Religiosen* (Einsiedeln, 1906), p. 137. It is significant that van Acken in his subject index has no entry for 'almsgiving', but one for 'collecting alms'.

4   Van Acken, *op. cit.*, p. 313; cf. p. 314; A. Tanquerey, *Précis de théologie ascétique et mystique* (Paris, 9th ed. 1924), pp. 246-7; E. Fehringer, *Ordensgeist* (Saarlouis, 4th ed. 1912), p. 163.

5   Cf. *Evangelica Testificatio* 20.

Ghislain Lafont

The Institution of Religious Celibacy

THE stability of the law is an index to the stability of society. If the law can be defined as the normative language of institutuons, then its formulation within a precise corpus implies a fairly clear awareness of the institutions themselves and of the global society wherein they operate. Periods of search of crisis or rebirth are not periods of rigorous codification. But this is no discouragement to jurists for whom it is an enthralling task to observe institutions in evolution and to coin provisional yet efficacious words to aid and abet such evolution. It is clear that through the voice of Vatican II the Church has brought about profound shifts of emphasis regarding not only its understanding of itself but also its relationship with changing modern society. Hence this is certainly not the moment for codification — neither for the religious life nor anything else. Which does not mean that we are in juridical wilderness and institutional anarchy; at any rate it should not mean it. But we are invited to return to the very roots of our institutions and simultaneously to observe the thoroughly contemporary form that they are taking. It is more or less to this task that I wish humbly to devote myself in this article, by attempting to explore the institutional levels of the religious life and starting out with the precise human situation known as celibacy. One can approach the question of the religious institution of celibacy through its directly ecclesial and charismatic aspect or one can approach it from the human, bodily angle (so to speak) where the highest values are clearly outlined. I am choosing the latter startingpoint here so that I can draw attention to various very concrete articulations in the religious life and the religious institution of celibacy — ones that all future juridical language will have to take into account.

49

I. THE CELIBATE LIFE AS INSTITUTION

Sometimes we have to emphasize truisms. We can certainly say that all values, human and religious alike, are common to everyone, to celibates as much as to others. But it is equally obvious that all values are not lived out in the same way but according to whether one is celibate or not. A celibate's personal psychology and insertion within society differ profoundly from those of a married person. Apart from all spiritual determination and all defined intention, there is a distance that we could call 'bodily' between the celibate and the married person in their approach to the world and to other people. Here I am using 'body' or 'bodily' to denote the reality in man through which mediation with the world takes place. This mediation is exercised in a fundamentally different way according to whether a man is married or not, that is to say according to whether he actualises or not what could be called the primary bodily relationships: namely, sexual relations (in the full sense of the term) with a person of the opposite sex, and parental relations with children. These primary bodily relationships in fact determine a basic social cell in function of which, as a result of which, or, simply, with which all other relationships are built, developed and lived — relationships with things as with people: professional life in its different aspects — technical, social, economic; interpersonal life at the level of encounter with other men and groups; symbolic life — leisure, games, culture, religion. Nothing of all this is lived without multiple reference to the social cell formed on the basis of the primary bodily relationships; in particular, the evolution of all this complex of relationships is conditional on a crucial element: the birth and growth of the freedom of the children.

A celibate's relationship with the world appears straightaway different, for the unmarried man does not actualize the two primary bodily relationships; he does not exercise the modality of being-in-the-world in which bodiliness is most immediately involved and where language is consequently at its most intimate. The celibate lives in an infinitely greater basic solitude, but because his solitude makes him more available his possibilities of encounter on other levels than the primary one are wider. Wider possibilities in what concerns the registers of profession, of encounter, of symbol, yes, but different possibilities, because they are produced by a humanly different situation. For myself I believe that it is at the 'primary bodily' level that the root of the traditional distinction between 'states of life' is to be found.

The point I am trying to make here is that celibacy is, of itself, a definite social institution, corresponding with and in contrast to the social institution of marriage and the family, the distinction and contrast coming from the different situations with regard to the primary bodily relationships. The personal and social economy of celibacy is always the same — whatever the motives or events that have led a man to embrace it — but it is always different from the economy of marriage. Levi-Strauss has touched on the question of the sociology of the celibate in what are called primitive societies; a similar sociology should be studied and elaborated in all its variants regarding the same man living in our own highly developed societies. In the matter of the specifically religious institution of Christian celibacy, we can, however, be sure that many of its traits are not specific to religion: they simply accord with the sociological truth of the institution of celibacy. From one point of view the organization of the religious life is identical to the organization of human life when deprived of the primary bodily relationships. In the measure that the sociological truth of an institution is a function of the conjuncture but also of the concept of man as a social being arrived at in any given civilization, in the same measure can the form of the religious institution be defined and lived. But the converse may equally be true — that the attempt to define the concrete form of the institution of religious celibacy at a given epoch may help every man, whether celibate or not, to discover the dynamic truth of his place within society.

So here we have a basic element — susceptible of analysis at its own level — in the definition of the nature of the institution of religious celibacy and eventually of its normative language.

II. THE DECISION FOR CELIBACY

The celibate life in our civilization is often a situation to be suffered. There is much to reflect on here if we were seeking to understand why, though we live in a society where there are large concentrations of people and where most of the obstacles to marriage (necessary in traditional society for its conservation and balance) no longer exist, there are nevertheless so many people who do not in fact get married. But. this is not our subject at the moment.

Celibacy, however, can also be a state of life that is decided on, chosen. Such a choice can, of course, simply depend on the inescapable fact that someone finds himself celibate because for various reasons he has not had the opportunities to be able to marry, so he 'takes on' the situation and tries to discover and live its dynamic meaning, for others and for himself. But there is also the case of a decision deliberately made (whether for a period or for ever) as a result of the variety of motives that can lead a man either to delay the establishment of the primary bodily relationships or to organize his life in some way definitely outside them. I want to suggest that these various motives can be grouped according to two distinct lines which we could describe as the 'professional' line and the 'monastic ' line — giving both terms a very general meaning.

There are, for instance, men who postpone marriage or renounce it because scientific research holds their entire attention; likewise a teacher can be so engrossed in his job that he decides not to marry so as to keep his educational powers free for the students who come to him; and likewise again many 'volunteers' in political, social or charitable action put off marriage till later so as to dedicate themselves more fully to their action. Examples could be multiplied. The important point here is that the decision in favour of celibacy has its institutional consequences, of which the most important is the special relationship (whether temporary or permanent) with the professional community (scientific, educational, field work) whose interests one shares, whose adherents one meets, whose aims one espouses. This special relationship is intrinsically qualified by celibacy and is all the more intense in that it is exclusive, for the participation of the celibate brings with it an availability of time, money and a freedom of mind that married people probably will not have. For the celibate, the well-known conflict between family and profession (in the widest sense of the term) is avoided, because one of the two elements does not exist.

Celibacy can also be deliberately chosen in the context that I have described as 'monastic', giving that word a meaning on a fundamental level that encompasses all philosphical or religious diversity. The aim probably being pursued in this case is the discovery of the truth of oneself by means of a process of withdrawal whose first stage is the adoption of celibacy viewed as the first step in establishing solitude. This is not the place to discuss various ambiguities inherent in a 'monastic' purpose of this kind. On the extremely broad level where we are now considering it, this type of celibacy is a fact sufficiently widely attested in the history and geography of civilizations for its authenticity to be generally acknowledged. This purpose, however, is not necessarily definitive and its realization does not necessarily entail entering a monastic institution in the strict sense. The permanence of the purpose and the conditions of its realization are dependent on the evaluation each man makes of himself and the conditions he considers necessary for the goal he is striving after: a better knowledge of himself, or inner liberation. Whatever its diversities, this monastic purpose involves a formalization of life and is equally the creator of a community; a community perhaps less characterized by the action pursued than by a similarity of outlook on life and a certain generality of the means employed. The frequent contacts in these last years between people of different confessional or philosophical allegiance, but with the same 'monastic purpose' in common, have revealed not only the institutional constants inherent in this purpose but also the points of encounter between the people or (strictly speaking) communities who pursue it.

As a result of this rapid analysis we can discern a second level in the institution of celibacy; a level that is linked to personal decision and brings with it an immediate special relationship with the community of those who, whether celibate or not, have made a similar choice. The institution of religious celibacy should pay the greatest attention to this level, especially where the 'professional' line is concerned. The problem could be formulated like this: what form can or should Catholic religious life take if it wants to respect and even favour special adherence to a professional community?

III. PROMISE AS INSTITUTION

Till now we have been considering celibacy as depending entirely on the situation, and/or the personal decision, of the individual; at this level it derives solely from his freedom which either consents to the situation or creates it by his decision. The particularity of community relationships remains on the horizon of the decision but does not constitute it. What I want to say now will become clearer if we take the case of the vowed celibate. The vow or promise involves two connected elements which modify fairly deeply the image of celibacy. To begin with, a promise is usually made to someone else. Of course one can promise something to oneself, but in this context only oneself is compromised (in any case this is an application derived from the notion and the word). A promise made to another compromises the other, in the sense that the situation it creates has repercussions on the life of the other, and this is precisely why it should be accepted. The situation thus created can from one point of view be called juridical, inasmuch as it creates a legal relationship between the people: if it is not a contract, because there are not strictly speaking reciprocal oaths, there is nonetheless a mutual commitment defining a present and a future through the fact of the promise and its acceptance.

The second characteristic of a promise is that it involves time and concretely pledges the future. In this it differs from mere decision. Decision too, of course, determines the configuration of time, because what I have decided to do, and what I accomplish with the passage of time, qualifies my duration. But so long as there has not been a promise nothing is formally binding on the configuration of time, a re-evaluation of the situation is still possible without any preamble, and a fresh decision can be taken in the opposite direction. But once there has been a promise and an acceptance, a certain provisional or permanent configuration of time has been fixed and determined, independently in a certain sense of developments to come. We usually say that a promise is kept; that means that the configuration of time which has been anticipated (put-in-advance, *'pro-mise'*) is respected in the manner in which it has been foreseen. Everything happens as though we know in advance that the vicissitudes of the future, whatever they may be, will never be such as to prevent time being given the configuration that has been decided on and prepared for.

Thus we see that by means of a promise a man puts himself in a sense above and outside the passage of time: as far as he is able and insofar as he is personally committed, he shapes the future configuration of time and does not anticipate that any other configuration could be substituted for it. It's a risk, but it is man's nature to take risks. At all events, we see dawning here a new component of what will be religious celibacy. In order to make a promise there has to be as it were an institution of the promise; methods of investigating the future, of reasonable prospecting; a pedagogy of commitment (linked to the nature of the commitment under consideration), hence an institution of dialogue. None of this is specific to religious celibacy but is encountered wherever there is human commitment: the processes of this institution of the promise, on both the psychological and sociological levels, will thus have to be studied and taken into consideration when we come to define the institution of religious celibacy.

IV. A CELIBACY PROMISED TO GOD

Looking at things from the point we have now reached, deliberate Christian celibacy is characterized by being celibacy promised to God. The partner of the promise is not a man nor a human community, but the true and living God. This element of the promise made to God is the common denominator of all forms of dedicated Christian life, from the most hidden and solitary to the most formal as manifested in a venerable Order. And I would now like to put forward one or two observations about this promise in itself, its necessary relationship with the Christian community, and the particular institutions it gives rise to.

The promise of Christian celibacy is not made to any god; it is not a commitment relating to the 'divine', nor a search for the divine dimension within oneself. It is a promise made to God, to God who was the first to promise and who has shown himself faithful to that promise: the personal God who manifests himself in the history of men. And if it is this God with whom we are dealing, the first thing to say is that a promise made to him does not, as it were, leave him unscathed. Whatever language we choose to say it in, the Christian message implies that there is a history of God. The question of knowing exactly how God is affected by our decisions as men is as difficult as that of knowing how he is affected by the act of Creation and the manifestation of Revelation; but the problems of language do not annul the truth of the fact. The promise of celibacy is not a decision without an opposite number, or to which the opposite number is impassive, in the sense this word has for us. Let us say, if we like, that the impassivity of God is passionate. Thus he accepts the promise. Thus the promise made to the living God and accepted by him creates a relational structure between God and man, mysterious but real, which commits the configuration of time and which we can for this reason qualify as an institution. To the theological hope of the Church, which is founded on God's promise to expect the Kingdom and to work for its advent at the heart of our expectation, there corresponds the hope of the man who has promised celibacy and lives under the driving force of God's acceptance: in both cases the configuration of time is fixed and determined and God's power expected and accepted.

It is in this perspective and in this one alone, it seems to me, that it is possible to understand the theme of a definitive promise, rather difficult though it be to admit today. The history of the Christian celibate is no different from that of every man: it involves many twists and turns, many evolutions, many modifications, that must moreover be lived within a certain steadfast fidelity to oneself. But because the Christian promise of celibacy is made to the living God and accepted by him, because it is founded on the divine promise and can be lived in hope, it can assume the character of finality (though it can also relate to some predetermined duration depending on the inspiration and decision of each individual). Thus it has in view the very mode of existence that one chooses to live before God and with him, and it is taken for granted that future developments will be integrated within this mode which has been chosen and promised as final. A kind of proof of this possibility is given us when we consider what I called earlier on the institution of the celibate life: time is irreversable, and celibacy of itself creates a personal and social situation that is defined, determined and unshakable. A life that starts out under the sign of vowed celibacy becomes 'embodied' within the world according to this definition and determination, and herein lies its irreversibility; the man, for instance, who embarks on marriage when entering his third period of life complies with the primary bodily relationships in a way which can hardly be called normal or customary. This sort of 'bodily' anomaly, resulting from a change in the state of life that was not originally foreseen, is perhaps a sign of the human truth of a definitive commitment taken vis-à-vis God.

V. CELIBACY WITHIN THE CHRISTIAN COMMUNITY

God is known as living and faithful and is called by his true name only within the community constituted by the confession of faith, which means the recognition of God's revelation. The Church was born of belief in God's fidelity, a belief that expresses itself in a structure of word amd institution. It is only within the community, drawn together through confessing God's fidelity, that there can arise the desire for a life united to the faithful God through a promise that pledges the form this life is to take. The Christian community is thus first and foremost the milieu that nourishes Christian celibacy.

If the confession of faith uniting the community proceeds from the Holy Spirit who alone causes God to be acknowledged as Father and Jesus Christ as Saviour, likewise the promise of celibacy addressed to the living and promise-giving God can only come from the Spirit; this is what is normally meant when it is said that celibacy is a charisma: 'bodily' reality, hence visible and witness-bearing, which through the personal commitment of a Christian signifies the total fidelity of the Church to the faithful Godhead.

Since it is within the Christian community that God is known by his Name and that the Spirit calls up a charisma of celibacy, this latter is doubly linked to the community. The personal institution, created by the promise made to God, exists only in the institution of the Church: the Christian community as depository of the Gospel is capable of discerning the truth of a purpose of Christian celibacy, of drawing it out, of receiving its public profession (under whatever form it is realized), and — this is essential — of testifying to the acceptance given by God of the purpose thus professed. This general relationship with the Church is completed, in the second place, by adherence to one of the groups that have charismatically arisen and been organized in the Church, and in which those who have vowed celibacy — following a diversity of inspirations and goals — are to be found. Moreover, it is usual for celibacy to be vowed only on condition of adherence to one of these groups.

This is not the place to go into detail concerning the institutions of the religious life in the Church. In the fairly wide scope of this article I would like to end up with two comments. In the first place I would like to voice a certain doubt regarding the capacity of the Christian community, including those hierarchically responsible for it, to release a man from a promise that was made to God. Can the mediation of the Church go so far as to annul a structure founded on a reciprocal pledge between a man and God? We can agree that the Church is competent to examine and determine whether a promise was ever really made with sufficient freedom and knowledge, and eventually to decide in favour of a nullity — to decide, that is, that the promise never existed. We can also agree that the Church can affirm that a man is no longer able or willing to remain in the state of life which was the object of a promise — and this, without bringing damaging judgment to bear and without excluding him from his communion. But can we go any further? If the promise made to God truly became an element in the history of man and God, if an agreement was concluded which implicated the Spirit of God and the deepest freedom of a man, who could, strictly speaking, 'annul' that?

If my first comment seems to press for the permanence and solidity of the basic institution created by the promise exchanged between man and God, my second tends perhaps to bring out the mobility 'of practice' (so to call it) of institutions. This mobility seems to me to be founded on respect for the various levels of the institution of celibacy as I have tried to outline them in this article. In a perspective of waiting for the Kingdom, the fact of having chosen celibacy by means of a promise made to God does not render those human levels inoperative, useless, null and void. The celibate consecrated to God should respect the truth of his insertion within society, according to the form of the contemporary world in which he is; it is also very possible that his activities have inserted him within human communities where he participates in his specific state as a man consecrated to the Kingdom and testifying – through sharing a same task – to God's fidelity and the finality of all things towards this Kingdom. We see here the immense flexibility that the institution of religious celibacy can allow for, in function not only of the particular spirituality or evangelical orientation of the person and the institutes, but in function eventually of the human commitments that can and should be made in all seriousness and loyalty with regard to men. We may even see diversities of orientation in the promise of celibacy itself; it can crown a decision of the 'professional' or 'monastic' type and this outcome at its own level comes first; but it can also come altogether first and later give place to types of commitment that will be taken on in function of the perceived urgency of the Gospel in the situation. The types of community, the practice of human relationships, personal and economic status – all this can vary very much as a result of the orientation that has been taken. More and more we seem to see a type of religious life in which a man, in agreement with those responsible but nevertheless in an autonomous and decisive way, discovers the orientation of his life and the choices to be made at the heart of his irreversible commitment *vis-à-vis* God; there is a personalization of life governing the concrete mode of the religious life. As for the communities themselves, the most lively are those which retain great flexibility yet steadfastly stake their all on the Christian and human truth of the religious life.

VI. CONCLUSION

What I have said is fragmentary indeed. My intention was primarily to outline a perspective, a way of approaching the religious institution of celibacy (in the most general sense of the term) which would take into account its human roots without in any way denying the promise made to God, the irreversible character of which I have on the contrary emphasized, inasmuch as the living God is the recipient of the basic institution which the promise creates. But it's a long haul from here to a more precise description of the religious institution in its personal and collective aspects, and from here to the elaboration of a fixed juridical formulation in words. But perhaps we should take the side of *not* belonging to the generation that can describe, fix and define. G. K. Chesterton's warning no doubt applies to us: 'When things go very wrong we need an unpractical man . . . A practical man means a man accustomed to mere daily practice, to the way things commonly work. When things will not work, you must have a thinker, the man who has some doctrine about why they work at all. It is wrong to fiddle while Rome is burning; but it is quite right to study the theory of hydraulics while Rome is burning.' (*What's wrong with the World*, 1910.)

Translated by Barbara Lucas

Tarsicius Jan van Bavel

Small Group and Big World

TO write about problems of structure in the religious life of today is a delicate business. The fact is that there are so many structures in the religious life: dependence on a centralized authority in Rome or on a diocese, democratic authority vested in a general chapter or the more monarchal authority of a general superior or abbot, election of the individual responsible over a limited period or from four to twelve years or an election for life, structures designed to ensure efficient work or structures to further an interpersonal common life, structures proper to s small or a large group. Then again, experience with these structures will vary from person to person. One will feel a given structure to be an obstacle to freedom, while another may feel deprived of anything to hang on to, when a structure disappears. It is asking for trouble even to venture a general statement that this or that structure may have a value or a useful purpose. One person will take this to be a defence of existing bad structures, someone else as evidence of a feeling that without a minimum of structures 'it won't do'. I have often found that female religious are more afraid of structures than the male ones are. Could this be because they have found them (or find them even now) more of a burden than men do?

I. THE SIGNIFICANCE OF A STRUCTURE

Let us first settle what we are to understand here by 'structure'. I would like to start from the broad meaning: a structure is any existing disposition or arrangement. The very fact that a structure already exists, is given in advance, detracts to a greater or less degree from my personal freedom. It is not my own 'free' project but that of others or even of a power above and beyond every one of us. Structures embrace and contain our lives in a much more incisive way than we might at first sight suppose. When we speak of structures, we think immediately of organization, a fixed network of governing authority, laws, rules and prescriptions. But in fact every surrounding circumstance is a structure: our language, our living accommodation, the lay-out of a building, the society and culture into which we are born, all that and much more are structures. I heard somebody or other say: the biggest structure is me. Indeed our own temperament and character are given factors that in large measure detract from our freedom, *a fortiori*, therefore, from the freedom of others. There are structures over which we have some hold; but there are others which we cannot possibly reverse or annul. So we should handle the slogan 'away with all structures' very cautiously indeed. At bottom that is a nonsense. Man needs structures to enable him to exist. It follows from what has been said above that there is a fundamental tension between structure and freedom. Up to a point a structure is always a constraint. A structure is also, by its very nature, invariably 'conservative'. Because of these properties it may well have the effect of smothering life or crushing a person. Charles Peguy says somewhere that the elementary word for freedom is 'disorder'; for freedom is never susceptible of being squeezed entirely into this or that framework; freedom needs room in which to be creative. Moreover, freedom allows free play to natural contrasts and to varying conviction. Letting somebody else have his freedom inevitably leads to pluriformity, to a recognition of the inequality of each individual (and every group) within the fundamental equality of all men. It hardly needs to be said that a structure which impedes and militates against freedom and stifles life is a bad thing. In such a case we are bound to intervene and engineer a change wherever this is possible.

Of course, there is still the problem of defining exactly at what point 'true' freedom and 'authentic' living come into all this. There are no universal norms here. But this is where the positive *raison d'être* of a structure becomes apparent. For though in one respect a structure may constrict our freedom, it does so in order to stimulate that freedom in another respect. If we had to structure our whole life creatively ourselves, from a to z, this would not only be an impossible task but would also result in the maximum of unfreedom. Ultimately, therefore, a structure must create more freedom, by presenting a framework to our freedom that is neither unlimited nor absolute. Thus we acquire a certain stroke in swimming, which is highly structured, so as to be able to move freely in the water; we conform to the structures in traffic so as to be able to travel freely from here to there; we accept the structures of language in order successfully to communicate with one another; we respect certain social structures in order to be able to live with other people.

Each structure must be constantly examined, therefore, for its 'freedom-value'. But it would be an illusion to imagine that a community could exist without any structure at all. Even in a marginal, free group spontaneous structures and sections emerge, if only because of the disparity and 'otherness-in-being' of the various persons involved.

II. PERSONALISM AND TOTALITY

Personality is a thing of prestigious worth. Over the centuries the effect of our culture has been to bring to the fore and protect the value of the individual person. Each person stands for something inalienable and irreplaceable. Everyone has a right to a life of his own, his own freedom and his own responsibility. These are never to be used by others as a 'means'. That would imply a direct attack on human dignity. What provides the rational ground for this at a deeper level is love. For 'to love somebody' – what else does that mean but to defer to the person beside me, to acknowledge his value and enable him to attain the full development of his unique selfhood, that is to say, his being-in-otherness? Love means helping another to grow in his consciousness, his freedom, his responsibility, his goodness. Love means to give life, in the many senses of the word 'life'. Loving is not just a biological process; it is also being happy, building something, putting up with setbacks and with suffering, being of significance to someone else, not being 'on one's own', being able to take pleasure in things, being in good heart, understanding and being understood, evincing confidence and faith, looking to the future and having hope, cherishing and being cherished in return. This is why lovelessness, indifference, lack of appreciation, distrust, the abrogation of freedom and abuse of power are so many acts of grievous assault upon the life of another person.

That is a common enough thing to say. The value of the individual person has come to be something we take for granted. And yet I see a danger in our current personalism. It too can be onesided; for the person is not just individuality, not just exclusive and private selfhood. That is indeed the person; but he is more – he is selfhood *in community*. We should not envisage the individual as an absolutely autonomous or independent being, divorced from the relation connecting him with other people. To forget that this selfhood, personal selfhood, forms part of a larger whole, that is, of mankind, is to ignore the real state of affairs.

The two aspects of our human mode of being – subjectivity and totality – are represented by H. Fortmann thus: 'there are two forms of consciousness: that of the distancing I and that of the blending process, that of individualism and that of unification. The I and the objectivizing knowledge proper to it yield stability and security. The letting go of the I is an adventure not without risk . . . One might sum it all up as the courage to lose oneself, to abandon oneself to something or other: to a person, to an activity that will absorb us, to what religion calls the Absolute or God . . . And to the one who lets himself go there is revealed a world other than the world we encounter in an active assault upon things as objects that we set over against us and then subdue.'[1] Is a choice of emphasis permissible here: that is to say, by giving precedence to either the value of the person or that of the totality? Is it a question of spirituality, according to whether one opts for the unique selfhood of the person as a supreme value or for the totality as the supreme value? We find in fact that some care more about the development of an individual's personality, others more about community, with a consequent degree of self-effacement. Or should both postures go together, in a harmonious union? To hold the balance between the two positions is certainly no academic issue: ordinary, day-to-day living shows how extremely difficult it is.

I would want to call rather more attention to the aspect of solidarity, because as I see it this complies best with the human impulse to love: being happy with and for one another; the greatest happiness is not individual happiness but being happy together. The final aim of love can never be the disappearance of the I for the sake of a larger whole – but it *is* the fullness of the I within the whole. I therefore do not see community just as a technical or functional requirement. In that case the community would be no more than a necessary evil or an exercise in ascesis. I regard the community as an integral part of the individual. What a person is he is in part through and in the community.

At present there are obvious signs of a change in the drift of western thought. Alongside the value accorded to personalism there is a growing awareness that personalism by itself is not going to see through. More than ever there is need for another way of thinking. For the first time in history the whole of mankind, the whole world and the cosmos itself have become our field of work. No one can confine himself any longer to the small circle of his own group, country, nation or race. Everything is bound up with the whole and has worldwide repercussions. Regional welfare and national justice are no longer able to answer all our questions; as soon as may be we shall have to achieve a welfare and a justice that embrace the world. Europe is being forced to surmount its fragmented nationalism and arrive at a genuine European community (however hard it may be get it off the ground!).

The United Nations and many other world organizations are so many attempts to achieve a new approach to mankind as a whole. What is evident from all this is an imperative need for a global, universal or corporative kind of thinking. One might even describe it as a thinking in terms of the totality or collective. What one calls it is neither here nor there; what is important is the thing itself. It calls for a radical change of outlook − and no one should underestimate this change in our mentality; it is a tall order for everybody, from north to south, from west to east.

Does all this mean that personalism will be crushed out of existence? I believe not. Personalism will still be needed to provide a basis for the whole. No whole can emerge without the person; and conversely, no person can exist without the whole.

III. SMALL GROUP OR WORLD ORGANIZATION?

Just as it is throughout present-day culture, the tension between personalism and totality is also observable within the life of religion. At the basis of the religious revival which at the moment is finding expression mostly in smaller groups there is a longing for genuinely personal contact, for a new form of living together. In the phenomenon of the small group one can see a protest, nay, even a kind of indifference, regarding the large anonymous network of inter-relationships of vast institutions. Nobody can argue that striving for authentic communication is not worthwhile. It discloses something of the tremendous need in our day for 'une chaleur communautaire', the need for human warmth. In new forms of shared living religious are searching for an answer to the excruciating isolation of modern man. Reciprocal trust and friendship serve to counterbalance an impersonal and bureaucratic society, of which their own institution often forms a part. Is it not the case that inspiration, creativity and freedom are to be found only in really living relationships? The ideal type of being and living in 'togetherness', however, makes very lofty demands of the individual person, such as: spontaneity, mutual solidarity, a spirit of sacrifice, personal knowledge of one another, combined reflection, a psychic oneness in evaluating, thinking and taking action.

The history of the religious life shows us that communities which are too big and powerful have in the long run not been viable and have tended to crumble from within. Of necessity a large group calls for more organization. Then the structures can be quite overwhelming in their effect and may very often stifle all inspiration. Quite recently R. Hostie showed that each new wind of inspiration in the religious life had blown itself out in a matter of 150 to 200 years.[2] What is new grows old and ceases to be challenging. The ideal loses its attraction and no longer stirs people into activity. It is at this juncture that structures become more important. Whereas previously it was the ideal itself that bound people together as a group and united them, now it is various organizational and disciplinary measures that become the factor making for unity. Where initially the ideal provided a clear basis for the group, that is now transferred to juridical rules. This kind of process is accompanied by a loss of spontaneity and freedom.

Surely that is the reason why again and again in the religious life people find it necessary to make a fresh start, and why they are constantly reverting to the small community? J. Leclercq says in this connection: 'If spontaneity disappears, if everything is minutely spelt out in writing, is catered for and controlled in a more or less bureaucratic way, monastic institutions may indeed survive . . . but no longer the spirit of monachism. Monachism will then inevitably reappear outside the institutions: ascetics, God-seekers living as individuals or in small groups, who have resumed their freedom *vis-à-vis* the corpus of legislation . . . When personal vocation is sacrificed to the institution, to the order, to the uniformity imposed by a detailed system of laws, then such a system is nothing more than a surrogate of a genuine, spiritual inspiration which it should really have stimulated.'[3]

The current preference for the small group creates tension in a number of orders and congregations. A lot of them are in fact international, worldwide organizations with a centralized administration, usually ensconced in Rome. At first sight one might suppose that this would work in favour of thinking in terms of totality. That might indeed be so; but experience suggests that often enough it is not the case. Where to look for the reasons why things go awry? They lie, I think, not only in the complex and often self-contradictory trends that bedevil our culture in these days, but also in the way authority is understood and exercised. A central governing authority is naturally bent on preserving a degree of unity; and so it opts, of necessity almost, for uniformity and for a way of ordering affairs that will apply to all and sundry. Uniformity of that kind, however, clashes directly with the freedom which is an essential component of the religious life. The religious life has always had a touch of the 'utopian' about it, something of the dream which can never quite come true, which means to improve upon things as they are and go far beyond them. And that cannot be poured into a fixed mould. To some extent, therefore, a utopia undermines all established forms of power.

IV. FREE UNDER GRACE

The world of the religious has always been a rather marvellous garden of freedom. The religious life has never been called into being from above by the official church authorities. It has invariably forced itself upon the hierarchy from below. The hierarchy has always taken a pretty negative view of every new religious movement to begin with, but in the end has been more or less liberal enough to let it carry on. During the last four hundred years, however, the Church's attitude has become set and much less flexible. The trauma of the Reformation, in particular, and the rapid changes taking place in the modern world have tended to give the Church a conservative character.[4] Distrust of freedom has grown considerably and has increasingly given rise to what one might call an 'anti' attitude. Instead of a positive attitude of being 'for something', a negative stance 'against this and against that' has predominated. Ecclesiastical administration reacts tardily, formally and in a legalistic spirit.

From the Congregation of Religious one expects rather more stimulus and encouragement. One cannot expect of a functionary that he should be an innovator; nor is that necessary. But one may well expect of him that he should stimulate, evaluate and encourage. With prohibitions and restrictions everything gets bogged down in negativism. The present time confronts everybody with large problems — not just the central authority, but every religious personally. Simply to shrug off the difficulties resolves nothing; better to face up to them together. Everyone must learn to accept the concrete world in which we now live, even if one is not entirely identified with it. At this moment of time the attitude of the hierarchy is often too far removed from the anxiety being felt at ground level. This difference is often the difference between conservatism and an open disposition, between slamming on the brakes and wanting to go forward. It is felt to be a lack of solidarity. People feel isolated and become indifferent to the centralizing authority. The documents emanating from a central authority should reflect something of a shared concern and solidarity, which at least afford some support in the search for solutions. Again authority should be open toward the future which none of us can anticipate and to which we are all of us on the way. A further growth of bureaucracy and institutionalism can only lead to a hardening of the arteries. Here it is worth reflecting upon what Anatole France once said: 'I prefer the mistakes of enthusiasm to the prudence of indifference.'

V. DEMOCRATIZING AND DECENTRALIZATION

Whether we like it or nor, the reins of control in modern society are obviously passing out of the hands of a tiny élite into those of ordinary people underneath. The professional and managerial sector used to include only five per cent of the population, while about eighty per cent were engaged in the activities of the labouring classes. In some parts of the world the proportion is now in inverse ratio: the service sector has increased to eighty per cent. This social revolution has consequences at every level of the community, the religious sphere included.[5] A small governing class can no longer think and take the decisions for the broad mass of people below them: that mass has achieved emancipation or is more and more intent on doing so. Communication is no longer confined to a group of 'insiders'. The business of the mass media is communication on a world scale; and they address themselves to each person's consciousness, judgment and responsibility. Something like that happens in the case of dialogue. Where in fact is dialogue carried on most effectively? Is it not in small groups at the popular level? It is there that people are in vital contact with one another.

This does not mean that the group has no need of authority. But one is of course bound to ask what sort of authority it does need. Evidently not one that takes no notice of personal freedom and issues orders from the top, not one that simply lays down the law, not one that rejects all criticism from below on the pretext that it must be subversive. No; what we want is an authority unafraid to engage in discussion and with something to say; an authority which understands that it is not there for its own sake but in order to represent and realize religious values.

Are the current structures of the religious orders and congregations sufficiently well adapted to cope with this revolution? I know of course that the process already described in outline is not everywhere equally far advanced, not even within one and the same group. I know too that the structures of orders and congregations did not spring up overnight but have been tried and tested over the centuries. Actually, the exercise of authority within the religious life can be reduced to two basic forms. In the case of the first one, the authority is in the hands of one or more general chapters, to which even the superior general is subordinate. The general chapter of Citeaux in the twelfth century has served as model for most of the orders. The second form leans more in the direction of a monarchal concentration of authority in a single leader. Here the organization of the Jesuit order has been the model for quite a number of modern congregations. Both forms had their advantages and their drawbacks. The chapter-form was certainly a democratic way of exercising authority but has in the past often been occasion for immobility and sterility. Even Citeaux grew tired of meeting, for several centuries. The monarchal form had the advantage that quick decisions could be taken, followed by immediate action. But where there was excessive centralization the whole thing became much too dependent on the leader's smallest foible; moreover, this system could easily lead to conformism, that is to say, to training and forming people without enough individual personality.

I have quite deliberately put the last few sentences in the past tense; for one may ask oneself whether the situation nowadays does not entail new terms of reference which cannot simply be assimilated by the existing structures. Huge enterprises often fall victim to their own unwieldiness. If it was difficult enough in the past to find capable leaders, are we not bound to say nowadays that in this complex and over-specialized world it has become just impossible for one person to take the measure of a larger whole. Setting up this, that and the other committee does not solve this problem. We all know how fed up people get with committees (which as a rule have no real authority) and how frequently they are just a cover for impotence and inefficiency.

Does not the very complexity of our times call for a wider distribution of real power? And since as we said earlier on authority is being virtually democratized, ought there not to be a commensurate decentralization of it? Should we not put more trust in and give more responsibility to the underlying stratum? In the world of politics one hears already here and there a demand for real proportional representation: one third men, one third women, one third youth. In so saying I remain fully aware that there are snags attaching even to the onward march of democracy — snags to which I have already referred elsewhere.[6] The crude law of the greatest number may easily become twisted into a refusal of obedience to the Spirit.

VI. POLARIZATION

Polarization is the most frightening thing in the modern world, including the religious world of the present day. By polarization I mean: ganging up against each other in groups because of an ideological difference of opinion. People entrench themselves in their own position, retreat inside their own theories and propositions and prefer not to listen any more to what the other side has to say. They accuse each other of being the cause of the prevailing crisis: if only everything had been left as it was, then there would be no question now of any crisis; if only the others would give way more and fall into line, then we would already be a lot further on and would have put a great deal of trouble behind us. Alas! polarization is tending to sharpen everywhere. Suspicion and insinuation are rampant; yet they are unworthy of the Church and threaten to degrade it into a police state.

Is polarization a transient phenomenon, an inevitable by-product of any crisis, and one that will disappear of its own accord? I do not know; I hope so. But it is certainly a source of tension, even of paralysis. Dialogue becomes a matter of talking past each other and in some instances no longer has any point to it at all. What one's approach should be when confronted with these acute forms of polarization it is not easy to say. Should we persevere in spite of everything with a group that is inwardly divided?

Does not the reason for the failure of so many general (and other) chapters also lie here? Of course they make it possible to differentiate more clearly between varying opinions; but often enough that fails to bring the participants one step closer together. It is a further question whether in such a situation general constitutions serve any real purpose. One person's need is not another's; what one may look for, another will not. The rapid developments taking place in our time do not come about everywhere at the same pace. The various stages of development have perhaps never been so diverse as they are today. That applies as much to individuals as to groups, as much to different countries as to different parts of the world.

Never has the need for international contacts been so great; but never have they been as problematical as in our day. In the history of the religious life there are examples enough of communities in which neither nationality nor race nor particularism played any significant role. These factors were no obstacle to the firmest cohesion. It would seem that the Middle Ages were more international than our own. Nationalism and particularism appear to have made their way into the religious life principally in the fifteenth century. But are nationality and race really the main restrictive factors at this moment? Is not the major one rather to be found in the polarization of beliefs and opinions. For one finds oneself perfectly *en rapport* with religious of another race or nationality provided one discovers in them a conviction and an ideal similar to one's own. Religious identify themselves in an identity of inspiration.

VII. CONCLUSION

In this article I have thrown up problems more often than I have proposed new ways forward. But those new ways may have to emerge out of the problems themselves. One might get the impression that I favour the small group. Does not that imply falling in completely with personalism and opting for isolation? Does it not mean surrendering altogether the dream of integration within the larger whole? I think not.[7] Perhaps we first have to rediscover the value of life in community and of really being together within a more miniature context so as to be able subsequently to grow toward that other stage of a worldwide connection (but then without western domination, of course). I fear that we are not yet ready for that. But time presses. New relationships within a world context should not be postponed for much longer if we want to avoid a global catastrophe. Helping to build a good community of human beings is therefore one of the most important tasks facing people in the religious life at the present time.

Translated by H. Hoskins

Notes

1   H. Fortmann, *Oosterse renaissance. Kritische reflecties op de cultuur van nu* (Bilthoven, 1970), p. 59.
2   R. Hostie, *Vie et mort des ordres religieux. Approches psychosociologiques* (Paris, 1972), pp. 82-3.
3   J. Leclercq, 'Le monachisme comme phénomène mondial', in *Le Supplément (La Vie Spirituelle)* no. 107 (1973), pp. 477-8.
4   L. Moulin, *Le monde vivant des religieux* (Paris, 1964), pp. 91-2, 99-113.
5   A. H. Smith, 'Theologie in de omkering van de beroepenpyramide', in *Kultuurleven* 40 (1973), pp. 1044-56.
6   Cf. my book, *De kern van het religieuze leven. Evangelische spanning die onze gemeenschap drijft* (Tielt-Utrecht, 1973), pp. 261-4, and L. Moulin, *op. cit.*, p. 183.
7   Although I do regard the small group as an attempt to achieve better inter-personal relations, it has to be firmly said that even within the small group such relationships do not come about automatically. Even in the small group the pressure on the individual person and his freedom can become excessive; then again, selectivity may be enough in itself to impede the formation of a genuinely human community. Cf. C. Pulles, C. van Boekel, 'Honderd religieuzen – honderd en meer zorgen', in *Ons Geestelijk Leven* 50 (1973), pp. 286-316, especially pp. 309-12 on the positive and negative aspects of the small group.

J. Beyer

The New Legislation for Religious

I. AN ORIGINAL AND ENLIGHTENED BLUEPRINT

THE subject I was asked to consider was the revision of legislation concerning religious in the Latin tradition, but judging from the new
orientation of the Code now in preparation,[1] we will no longer speak of
legislation for religious, but for institutes of perfection — for all societies that is, of shared life consecrated by profession of the evangelical
counsels.[2] This change requires us to adjust to a new understanding of
the whole question.

Where St Thomas, in his teaching, canonized the term 'religious', the
new Code wil emphasize the practice of the counsels as the basic principle of life. While this manner of life still finds expression in a variety
of canonical institutions: orders, congregations, societies of common
life, secular institutes and other forms of consecrated life in community, the new Code, in the spirit of Vatican II, will emphasize the essential spiritual reality of the consecrated life rather than the institutional
forms in which it has expressed itself up till now and which were listed
above. This will make is possible to remain faithful to the Spirit who
blows where he will. In any case it is impossible to predict what new
forms of evangelical life will be raised up in the Church by God's gift,
but the new Code can at least create favourable conditions for their
acceptance.

II. AN IMPORTANT TEST CASE

With Vatican II a new perspective was opened up, favouring greater
fidelity to charismatic gifts, greater respect for the moral and physical

rights of individuals, a more positive attitude of openness to initiatives prompted by the Spirit.

Consecrated life has moved beyond the observances of the monastic order, opening up to include new forms of apostolic life,[3] of which the clerks regular were, for a long time, the most significant group.[4] From the 16th century onwards it embarked on a more adventurous phase of its evolution,[5] which only succeeded in establishing itself at the time of the French Revolution − and which received its official approbation in 1947 with the promulgation of the Apostolic Constitution *Provida Mater Ecclesia*, the charter of the secular institutes. This approbation was somewhat belated and did not exactly produce a new lease of life, but rather incorporated the results of much patient effort into the context of the Church's adaptation to modern times. It does seem that the Church could shorten these delays, if only its legislation would explicitly recognise this constant reality of ecclesial life: *the appearance of new forms of consecrated life*.

From this point of view it can be argued that the schema on the consecrated life is an important test case − it could be the sign of the new outlook that was called for by Vatican II and which must now be realized in the life situation.

The study group which prepared this schema produced something of an innovation, which was discussed in the reports published in *Communicationes*,[6] and praised for its high quality and its frankness. In fact the schema introduces a new concept, and a flexible outline of what the consecrated way of life could be in the Church. The reports already published possess the merit of having laid down the principles which guided the drafting of these canons; they show the respect with which one would like to surround the spiritual inheritance of so many institutions which, once freed from the grip of a common law that is too detailed and too uniform, will be able, for the first time perhaps, to return to their sources by providing themselves with structures which respond to their original inspiration, to their particular charism, to the views of their founders. It was precisely this that the Code of 1917, which merely restated the majority of the 'Normae' of 1901, had prevented; the 'Normae' themselves had already given a strongly uniform character to the rules of religious congregations.

III. THE MAIN DIVISIONS OF THE SCHEMA

The law for institutes of perfection − and the name itself is not acceptable, calling to mind as it does that other controversial expression, 'states of perfection' − is presented in the following way.[7]

Part I, concerned with all forms of consecrated life, treats of the approbation and organization of these institutes, their relationship with the hierarchy, and their government, both spiritual and temporal; it moves on then to the question of the recruitment and formation of members, the commitment they make, and the rights and duties that derive from it; and finally it discusses the question of those who break their ties with the institute, either by entering another or by leaving – of their own choice or because they have been dismissed. These norms, which are applicable to all, provide a basic legal framework which prescribes nothing or almost nothing, but invites institutes, in their own legislation, to specify the particular features which the traditional demands of all community living assume there.

Part II, which is entirely new, should be regarded as something special: it groups institutes according to the way the Spirit acts in them; it affirms the overriding importance of the legislation proper to each group, its twofold character, spiritual and juridical; in a few clauses it defines the fundamental characteristics of religious life (the term is retained here), speaks highly of the eremitical life, and then proceeds to look at the great traditional forms of consecrated life: monks and nuns; the rich variety of institutes dedicated to the apostolate; canons regular; conventual institutes of the mixed life where an attempt is made to harmonize monastic observance with the demands of some apostolic work which, of necessity, is not full time; and apostolic institutions in the fullest sense ranging from the clerks regular to the most recent foundations. Then come 'societies of the common life' which the Code had tried to assimilate to religious institutes while leaving them a large measure of freedom – a freedom which was advantageous to them.[8] The best-known of these societies is the Society of the Sisters of Charity founded by Saints Vincent de Paul and Louise de Marillac, while the Lazarists, the Eudists, the White Fathers, and the many societies of secular priests who formed themselves into groups in order to go out as missionaries, should also be mentioned. These societies were not 'religious' and did not wish to be. All the same, the community life, the shared ideal and the difficult mission they undertook were translated into norms of living which were inevitably inspired by the Gospel, the three counsels, and religious observances. It is unimaginable that it might have been otherwise.

The reflection which was provoked by the need to draft new constitutions, better adapted to the aspirations of these institutes, will be able to guarantee them a new lease of life. Delivered from the threat of being trapped once again in the detailed and uniform canonical framework of religious life, as interpreted by the Code of 1917, they will be able to recognise that they are something more than a mere association of secular priests, and that the mission which brought them together has also shaped them as apostles according to the communitarian norms of the consecrated life lived out in a group. The proposed title for these societies is: 'Institutes of apostolic life in community' (Instituta vitae apostolicae consociatae); the term has the advantage of drawing attention to their particular origins and purpose: to come together for the sake of a common apostolate. Any society which did not have the three counsels as its rule of life would find another place, canonically speaking, in the new Code and — as the report of the study group indicates[9] — would no longer be included in the schema. Finally, the schema will consider the secular institutes. Only recently approved, these last comers are still in the process of searching — a doctrinal search which produced theological reflections of which Vatican II was to make use in order to define better the secular character of the Christian laity; a search for structures, which they want to be as simple as possible so as to guarantee a genuine evangelical way of life, with increasingly normal contact with the world. This work purifies such institutes of any elements which simply imitate the apostolic religious life, while in their attempts to discover their own identity, they oblige religious institutes to affirm more clearly the public nature of their own witness through their life and action both in the Church and in the world.[10]

This is the pattern which underlies this important section of the new legislation entitled 'Institutes of perfection'. They could have adopted the title suggested at the time of the council: 'Of those who profess the evangelical counsels' or some other title which would reflect more adequately the real nature and aspirations of these institutes.

IV. THE MAIN PRINCIPLES OF THE NEW LEGISLATION

The principles set out in the first report on the drafting of this schema,[11] can be reduced to a single norm, namely, that *each institute has the right and duty to be faithful to its own charism, to its authentic traditions, to its mission in the Church*, which means ensuring that particular legislation takes precedence over general legislation as interpreted in the existing Code, or better, it means drawing up general legislation which respects the variety of life-style and freedom of action in these institutes.

This fundamental principle is expressed concretely in the four following observations:

1. General legislation, even while it recognises the charism of the consecrated life, cannot fully define it. In fact, law cannot express everything about the life, but it must serve as a reflection and a safeguard of it. Hence fidelity to the rule — general or particular — will still not be the same thing as fidelity to one's vocation, as the full realisation of the latter, as the norm of Christian perfection. According to this principle, the legislation proper to these institutes of consecreated life must take into account the personal vocation of their members and the dynamic quality of this way of life which is both a response to the divine call and a commitment in the Church. Rightly interpreted, this principle should make any kind of legalism impossible, as much in the life of the institutes themselves as in the personal strivings of their members.

2. *General legislation must recognise and safeguard the personality of each institute, leaving it free to express its own inner reality.* Once the fundamental principle which recognizes the charismatic nature of the consecrated life has been accepted, it no longer presents any problem. It gives the new legislation its special character – that of continually referring back to the rule proper to each institute; it turns the schema into a 'legal frameowrk' and justifies the guiding principle which underlies the second part of this schema: that institutes should be classified according to their own special vocation, the major characteristics of their ecclesial mission defined and their continuing existence in the Church in this way assured.

3. *While defining what is essential, general legislation must remain suffciently flexible to allow that the ideal of all life consecrated by profession of the counsels should be expressed, without coercion or strain, in the legislation proper to individual institutes.* The essential feature of all consecrated life is the dedication of oneself to God and men in union with the Eucharistic offering of Christ to his Father for the salvation of the world. This is the fruit of the entire tradition which, starting with the apostles, the consecrated virgins, the monks of the desert and the hermits, has lain at the heart of this way of life freely given under the inspiration of the Spirit. Gradually the Church singled out the three counsels, poverty, chastity and obedience, for any who would follow Christ and imitate as closely as possible his self-surrender to the Father and the total gift of himself for the life of all men, his brothers. The two commandments of Christian love thus form the central axes of the profession of the counsels and the latter express all its filial intensity in Jesus Christ.

As to the way in which the counsels are to be lived, everything will depend no longer on the legislation of the Church but on the gifts of the Spirit, recognized and authenticated by the hierarchy. The distinction between solemn and simple vows should not be retained in the general legislation. The poverty of the monk will be more uniform than that of the apostle; the chastity of the solitary knows other demands than those made on a consecrated person living 'in the world'; monastic obedience regulates the hours and days of the common life, while the obedience of the apostle is directed towards a particular mission, and is in keeping with the talents and initiatives involved in a personal and responsible apostolate. All these concrete expressions of the same evangelical counsel serve to bring out its depth and richness, increasing its witness value in the Church, where some of the faithful feel more attracted by Franciscan poverty, strengthened by the peaceful celibacy of the enclosed contemplative, or inspired by the responsible obedience of an institute dedicated to the apostolate; nor should the importance assumed today by the practice of the counsels in the midst of the world, in the secular institutes, be overlooked.

There are other characteristics common to institutes of consecrated life which are likewise a response to the counsels of the Lord, counsels which easily find some form of concrete expression in community life, for example, or in prayer and collaboration. The new legislation treats this last aspect as a point of particular importance. The founder's charism is indeed a gift of the Spirit, but it does not stop short at the person of the founder; it is extended to all those who at any time are called to live according to his rule, his constitutions, his spirit, and who will continue to carry out his work and mission in the Church. Union of hearts does not seem to necessitate living in the same house, which is normal for religious, nor does it require the community prayer essential to the monastic tradition. In each institute unity must discover its own forms of collaboration and participation, which are the first outward signs of fraternal charity. In this connection, institutes should concentrate on strengthening the main lines of their spirituality and bring out the evangelical nature of certain characteristics which might otherwise have been interpreted as mere social requirements.

4. In virtue of the grace which unites them, institutes of consecrated life, and above all those that live in community, must be encouraged in the general legislation to foster union of heart and mind. This principle is derived from the collective nature of the original charism. In their more faithful, more generous imitation of Christ, all share the same grace, the same gift. Those who live in community — and this form of life is essential to their public witness — are called to promote unity through collaboration in the works of the apostolate and to play a more responsible part in the allotting of tasks, the making of decisions, and the encouragement of initiatives — quite a considerable programme. Here again, however, too much uniformity could harm the particular character of certain institutes. Not all have a developed capitular form of government; some are very centralized; and on this point the schema does not impose any specific form of government, but leaves everything to be defined in the particular rule of each institute.

It is in this same spirit that the other guiding principles of the schema may be understood:[12] recognition that institutes of consecrated life differ from one another in kind, which is recognized by the special section of the schema; suppression of all distinction between men's and women's congregations. In the spirit of Vatican II it was essential that a stand should be taken on this point, while leaving women's congregations free to maintain certain traditions and options. It will be difficult, I believe, to free women's congregations from some degree of subordination, above all at the diocesan level, and in connection with dependences of a particular kind, such as that of the monastic 'second order' which depends on an institute of the mixed life. It should be noted, however, that the fundamental unity of the Carthusian Order, where monks and nuns form a single institute, should be preserved, as should the dependence of Cistercian nuns on the General Chapter of Citeaux. In such cases, by pushing the autonomy of the female branch too far, one runs the risk of depriving it of its vitality and spiritual strength. In the spirit of the schema, the solution to the problem must be found in the rule proper to the Order, and not depend on external intervention.

Finally, a brief look at two points which need not detain us here: the work of the study group has always sought to foster this growth of harmony between general and particular legislation — a delicate task which will have to be undertaken by all those involved in the drafting of constitutions for institutes of consecrated life. This harmony, moreover, will only be possible of the competent authorities too respect this spirit when they are asked to approve the text. It is based on the dignity of the individual, and his right to free association in the Church, and on the respect due to the action of the Spirit. It is, moreover, this very dignity of the individual person which the schema wishes to highlight: to remain faithful to the nature of the consecrated life as a divine cell, a personal vocation, legislation, both general and particular, must safeguard and define the rights of the person who has committed himself to it. Only too often it has been deemed necessary to stress first the obligations of the consecrated life, on the assumption that the consecration itself, as a 'deditio' to the Church, placed the members of these institutes in a state of 'servitude'. (Juridically speaking, this will have been inspired by Roman law.) This attitude has obscured the value of a life which gives itself without losing sight of its dignity and its rights. Some Christians, and some priests, have frequently assumed that to consecrate oneself to God was equivalent to placing oneself at the disposal of the clergy. Hence the abuses with which we are familiar and of which women's congregations were the principal victims.

V. CLASSIFICATION OF INSTITUTES

As the report on this schema made clear, a new and original section will treat the different types of consecrated life.[13] Already the decree, *Perfectae Caritatis*, had classified the different forms of consecrated life according to their different charisms: monastic life (art. 7), apostolic life (art. 8), and secular institutes (art. 11).

This is the perspective within which the study group carried out its work. The second part of the schema – some forty canons in all – classifies these different kinds of life and determines their particular characteristics. It complies very particularly with the desire of monks that their way of life should be better respected in the new Code. In fact the present Code was principally inspired by the apostolic type of community life in congregations with simple vows. The schema will, I believe, respond to this desire, but it will not provide a complete monastic rule; some points were developed in more detail, but such legislation would, in its own way, have constituted a fresh obstacle, as much for the life of existing monastic orders as for those new foundations now growing up in the Church.

Another well known desire has been dealt with in this schema: that the *statute for hermits* should be defined. Men and women of the desert are numerous today.[14] Some are members of a monastic order, others were originally active in the life of the apostolate; all retain their religious profession, but live it out in silence and solitude as hermits. This trend is not new in the Church; it has been very strong in recent years, and the desire, expressed during a number of renewal chapters, to found 'houses of prayer' belongs within the same spiritual movement.

There remains the case of the diocesan priest or the lay person who becomes a hermit. Will they be 'religious'? According to the present Code, in order to be one it is necessary to be a member of an institute approved by the Church. In view of this one can understand the desire of some hermits – I myself know of several – who would like to make profession of the counsels in order to consecrate themselves definitively to God. Can they not be recognized by the Church as religious? It would be strange if the most radical form of monastic life, that which is, to a large extent, the source of all consecrated life, should no longer be accepted in the Church today. The Council made a timid allusion to this way of life which is so much appreciated in the Eastern tradition. Yet there is no apparent reason why a Christian who dedicates himself to the eremitical life and makes profession of the evangelical counsels, should not be recognized by the Church as 'religious' and live in dependence on an abbot or a diocesan bishop who would approve his personal rule of life.[15]

What can be said in general legislation on the subject of monks that will not prejudice the variety of their different ways of life in the process? In the west we have Carthusiasn, Cistercians, the different Benedictine congregations, and other institutes, less well known perhaps, but which live faithfully according to their monastic ideal. And along with the monks there are the nuns – Benedictines, Cistercians, Carthusians, Carmelites, Poor Clares and many others, including those of recent foundation. The Council defined their way of life as an existence dedicated uniquely to the things of God in solitude and silence, in a spirit of persevering prayer and joyful asceticism, by which they offer to God an outstanding sacrifice of praise and give to the people of God an example of holiness and of hidden apostolic fruitfulness.[16]

The law of the Church, while praising such an ideal of life, can safeguard its autonomy, encourage easier movement from one monastery to another, give prominence to the idea of a special liturgy, recognize the duties and rights of the abbot or prior of the monastery, their powers of jurisdiction in particular cases, and recall the enclosure requirements proper to each institute.

Distinguishing their own way of life from that of the monks, the *canons regular* asked for reaffirmation of their own ultimate goal, of their solemn liturgy, of their pastoral activity in the vicinity of their abbeys, and of the possibility of federation while the autonomy of individual monasteries or congregations is preserved.

As for the *mendicant orders* (St Thomas called their life 'mixed'), the Council drew attention to their particular circumstances. While no longer stressing mendicancy as the primary characteristic of their ecclesial mission, the schema underlines — to judge from the outline plan of this second section — the community aspect of the 'conventual' orders. They were already preoccupied with the question of their own identity long before the Council,[17] and the latter urged them to remain faithful to their constitutions, 'combining the apostolic life with office in choir and monastic observances' while taking into account the demands of the apostolate. Such a way of life makes it difficult to engage in a full time apostolate, and this gives rise to a widely-experienced source of tension, especially among the young, who find that the monastic aspect emphasized during their early formation does not correspond to the concrete demands of their apostolic life. Each institute has been obliged to reconsider its original ideal: some have abandoned Office in choir in favour of common prayer; others will take a second look at the forms of their apostolate, which is often parochial and no longer allows for the solitary, silent life secured by the traditional observances.

The other *apostolic institutes*, especially those of women, must take care to preserve the balance, presupposed by their constitutions, between spiritual life and apostolate. As far as the latter are concerned, the schema can, I feel, do no more than reiterate the expressed wish of Vatican II that 'just as their whole religious life should be imbued with the apostolic spirit, so their apostolic activities must be shaped by the particular spirit of their institute.' Indeed — and the fundamental nature of this fact becomes increasingly apparent — the apostolate is no mere appendage to this type of religious life, but belongs to the very nature of such institutes; moreover, they were founded first and fore-

LIBRARY
KENRICK SEMINARY
7800 KENRICK ROAD
ST. LOUIS, MISSOURI 63119

most to carry out that apostolate for which their special charism set them apart. After dealing with these institutes, the schema turns its attention to the societies of the *common life* and *secular institutes* which I mentioned above.

So this restrained piece of legislation, which goes straight to the essential, will make it possible to fit charisms that have been received and new foundations into their place within the overall context of the consecrated life. Seeing the variety of constitutions and the flexibility of these norms, one can hope that every form of consecrated life will find its place within that context. This would allow one — which would be a good thing — to regard the classification of institutions not as a harking back to the past but as an indication of the outward structures which express the charisms of the consecrated life: monastic, mainly contemplative; apostolic, with its varying degrees of activity; and consecrated life in the world, which, in following its particular way, does well to emphasize its secular nature, and not rely unduly for inspiration on observances of the monastic or religious type.

Thus, the new legislation abandons historical labels, in order to recover the spiritual values proper to this state of life.

CONCLUSION

What is to be concluded from all this? The schema on 'institutes of perfection', provided it is accepted and understood in the spirit which produced it, will foster the full development of the consecrated life in the Church. It assures it of the possibility of following its own grace, its charism. This charism is not hierarchical, yet it is still a constituent element of the Church. Apart from a few general and, moreover, formal elements, it remains impossible to provide any healthy legislation which is uniform in this respect. The local Church, the parish and the Christian apostolate come into another category. Their life has given them a common appearance; their legislation is less diversified and more concerned with questions relating to organization. This is not so in the case of the consecrated life, which encompasses every aspect of the lives of its members, and has its own characteristic mission, outside the ordinary hierarchal framework.

When it is presented to the bishops and their advisers for discussion, the schema will provoke a certain measure of astonishment. Some will find it too open; others may not perhaps appreciate its originality; not finding it sufficiently 'canonical', some will want to make it more detailed, with greater binding force. In short, it will be a test case. Some superiors prefer to entrust to the prescriptions of the law all that they cannot obtain through the exercise of their authority, by respecting the rights of individuals.

As for the value of this text on the work of codification that is going on, the opinion of Fr Huizing seems apposite: 'The schema is the first to rethink these matters in depth; of all those I know, it harmonizes best with the spirit of the Council.'

Translated by Sarah Fawcett

Notes

1   *Communicationes*, 1 (1969), pp. 111-2.
2   *Perfectae Caritatis*, 1, d.
3   The first were the mendicant orders, Franciscans and Dominicans.
4   St Ignatius Loyola deliberately broke with all monastic observance.
5   Angela de' Merici, Foundress of the Ursulines, founded in Brescia in 1535.
6   *Communicationes*, 2 (1970), pp. 168-81; 5 (1973), pp. 47-69.
7   On this point see *Communicationes*, 2 (1970), pp. 173-6; 5 (1972), pp. 63-63-9; my own essay, 'Où en est la réforme du Droit canon? Les instituts de vie consacrée', *Vie Consacrée*, 43 (1971), pp. 291-3; and 'De Institutorum vitae consacratae novo iure', *Periodica*, 63 (1974), pp. 148-53.
8   See 'Les Sociétés de vie commune', *Gregorianum*, 48 (1967), pp. 747-65.
9   See *Communicationes*, 5 (1973), p. 51, n. 6.
10   I refer readers to my own study 'Critères de sécularité', *L'année canonique*, 17 (1973), pp. 93-106.
11   *Communicationes*, 2 (1970), pp. 170-3. See my article in *Vie Consacrée*.
12   I draw special attention to these in my article in *Vie Consacrée*.
13   See *Communicationes*, 2 (1970), pp. 175-6; 5 (1973), p. 67.
14   M. le Roy Ladurie, *Femmes au desert* (Paris, 1971).
15   See *Lumen Gentium*, 43, a; *Perfectae Caritatis*, 1, b; as well as *Unitatis Redintegratio*, 15, d, on the subject of monastic spirituality.
16   Pope Paul VI recalled this ideal when he spoke recently to the Congress of Benedictine Abbots (*AAS*, 55 (1973), p. 549).
17   See *Cahier des Ordres mendicants par la commission des O.M. de l'assemblée des Supérieurs Majeurs de France* (1965).

Robert Soullard

The Future of the
Religious Life

RELIGIOUS life will be what religious make of it. Can one, on the basis of the way they live today, get some glimpse of tomorrow's realities? Obviously it is not easy to give a developed answer to such a question. When one is speaking of the religious life, one needs to bear in mind the numerical importance of religious and religious institutes, as well as the very great variety of life-styles and stages of evolution. It is in the light of this complexity that one must interpret the living forces of the present and evaluate what they promise for the future.

My own reflections will be confined to the French situation, as being the only one with which I am familiar and in which one comes up against the difficulties of interpretation indicated above.[1]

II. INFLUENCES THAT HAVE AFFECTED DEVELOPMENT TO DATE

(a) It has become a commonplace to say that the present stage of development in the religious life began with the renewal chapters called for by the motu proprio *Ecclesiae Sanctae* of 6 August 1966. An initial assessment of these chapters was made in 1970, for a dozen or so men's congregations established in France, in a collection of articles published as *Leur Aggiornamento*.[2] More recently, in January 1973, J. Beyer SJ provided a more comprehensive and general survey in *La Nouvelle Revue Théologique*.[3] The problem set before these chapters, whose principal function was the drafting of new constitutions, is no longer entirely relevant to the present situation: now it is a question above all of evaluating the current state of affairs and preparing for the future in spite of unavoidable liabilities.

(b) If the drafting of constitutions which express what the religious life is corresponds to a stage that has been partly superseded, this is because a great deal has been written about the religious life, and because the influence of the authors has been considerable. I do not propose to list these works, even the most important. They are reported and analysed regularly in the various journals.[4] A renewed theology of religious life now exists, and it is widely known. A large number of constants emerge from these pieces of research, in spite of differences of approach − whether, that is, they refer back to the essentials of a tradition waiting to be renewed by the breath of the Spirit, or else concentrate on changing circumstances and on the demands of the contemporary world.[5]

(c) It is worth noting that the more direct intervention of certain theologians in matters connected with the religious life has tended to be in support of joint research and has provided an orientation for the efforts that will be required for the future. As far as the religious life of women in France is concerned, it is undeniable that the contribution made at the Assembly of the Union of Major Superiors in France (USMF) in 1971, by J. M. Tillard OP, one of the most frequently quoted French-speaking theologians of the religious life, was of paramount importance.[6]

(d) A determining factor for future orientations was the sociological survey on Religious Women in France initiated by the USMF and carried out by A. Luchini OP of the Centre Economie et Humanisme. This survey has just been brought up to date to cover the past three years. The summaries which appeared in 1970 undoubtedly constituted, at the time, an achievement that was unique of its kind.[7] The updating of the survey, with the addition of more precise facts about new foundations, underlines the consequences of obsolescence in existing institutes (a decrease of more than 10,000 religious), and emphasizes the continuing lack of recruitment − there is a proportionately greater number of entries into the contemplative life; but at the same time it draws attention to the vitality of an ecclesial institution in which the number of new foundations − often of an entirely new type − is almost equal to that of the closures.

II. EMPHASIZING COMMUNITY VALUES

Among the essential features of the development of religious life, the universal emphasis on community values must take the first place. The rich experience of the past allows one to expect the emergence of new forms for the future; but it should also be pointed out that many questions still remain to be answered.

(a) After a period in which the religious lived out his consecration in ascetic and individualistic perspective, the fact that religious life, which is intimately linked to the mystery of the Church, depends in some essential way on community life, was the great discovery of the post-conciliar period. Attention has been drawn to this, and in a masterly way, by J. M. Rillard in two articles published in the *Nouvelle Revue Théologique*.[8] This new understanding has resulted in a decrease in the number of large communities and the foundation of numerous groups of more restricted size or fraternities. Life in a small community satisfies, in fact, the desire for a more truly fraternal life, for a right appreciation of interpersonal relations, for a simpler life-style and for greater contact, not only between members of the community, but even more — and often above all — with the human milieu in which it is situated. The community is no longer turned in on itself, and, compared with the traditional type of community, it seems to have become fragmented, since it is no longer the only locus for prayer, encounter and companionship. 'Anyone who wants to preserve the ideal of the *koinonia*, which is essential to the experience of religious life, must of necessity foster or discover those intenser moments in the rhythm of community life which are no longer a regular daily feature. A new vision must replace the concept of community as something strictly localized and continuous — living together in the same place. The fraternity will find its meaning and the nourishment it needs in particular, intensely experienced moments rather than by living together and carrying out certain actions in common.'[9]

The religious has many relationships outside his community; sometimes, individually or with other members of his group, he may even join some grass-roots community or another form of mixed community — constituted, that is, of religious and lay people, men and women. There is a community of this kind at Ste-Baume (Var). The experiment, which is a typical French example of the new tendencies, is not without its difficulties.[10] It is therefore hard to say how far the desire to transcend the separation between the two categories — religious and laity — in a joint enterprise will find that the actual conditions favour the multiplication of such groups. In the meanwhile, many existing communities, in so far as they live in a spirit of truly evangelical openness, find in many cases that they constitute the most clearly perceptible concretisation of the community movement of today.

(*b*) Not all the findings of the first survey of experiments in community living are positive. In fact it raises many questions, about the present and with regard to the future. Jean Isaac OP, in his book *Réévaluer les voeux*, even speaks of a disaster that we must have the courage to acknowledge.[11] He argues that 'to try to remedy the present disastrous situation by improvising groups which lack guiding principles and are left at the mercy of the HLM[12] market without any spiritual support is both unrealistic and hypocritical.'[13] And without dramatising Fr Beyer has made similar statements.[14] As these authors make quite clear, small communities are not a recent discovery; but it is certainly true that what is rightly called the mystique of community is a new phenomenon. One should probably agree with Fr Isaac that insufficient attention has been paid to what he calls 'grace and mission' and to the creation of community structures with them in view.

(c) It will no longer be possible to evaluate the circumstances of an increasing number of religious, men and women, according to the traditional norms, which are still those embodied in the present legislation. There are widespread signs of a certain element of agitation, both in individual provinces and in institutes in general. Many religious find it difficult to capture any really concrete sense of their solidarity with their institute. Even more than by the number of departures, one is struck by the number of those who are living alone outside the community. This is something which is more keenly felt by women religious who, until now, have been accustomed to a very strict interpretation of the common life. No allowance is made within the framework of current legislation on exclaustration for the problems, aspirations and searchings of many religious.

(d) Some solitaries are so voluntarily, by vocation. These are the hermits, and their number is by no means negligible. In a fine, well-documented book, Marie le Roy Ladurie introduces these 'women in the desert'.[15] The present form of the eremitical life is something new in the history − the recent history, that is − of the west; it seems destined to survive and indeed to develop. But legislation has provided no adequate framework to date, especially where it is a question of hermits coming from the monastic life, who have frequently had no alternative but to return to their monastery or apply for an indult of secularisation.

III. TOWARDS WHAT KIND OF PRESENCE?

(a) The need to be present in the world in order to accompany contemporary man in his 'search for meaning' is a powerful driving force in the current evolution of the religious life, and has contributed in a big way to its changing physiognomy. Nor is the apostolic life the only one concerned; the contemplative life too has no meaning except in relation to the believing life of the Church as a whole.[16] Some attempts, timid as yet, have been made, not only to make the enormous communities which are found in most monasteries less cumbersome, more open − and there have been some real successes here − but also to ensure that the contemplative life is present in the new towns which are growing up alongside the major cities. Clearly the longing of our contemporaries for silence and a return to nature would seem to ensure some chance of success to monastic foundations buried in the depths of the country; but are we simply to resign ourselves to the idea that the contemplative life is only possible — often for reasons of strict enclosure — for communities which do not belong to the ancient orders (which nevertheless possess a rich and irreplaceable experience)? Several bishops have asked the question, and in their pastoral concern, they are only echoing the questionings of many adherents of the monastic life, not to mention the reflections contained in such works as those of Bernard Besret or Olivier du Roy.[17] Although of recent origin, the Fraternities of Bethlehem draw on the experience of the monastic orders and give concrete expression to these aspirations in particularly significant ways.[18]

(b) In the apostolic form of life, contact with the world is normally achieved through professional work. To have a profession is not something new for religious women as it is for members of the men's clerical institutes. But the professional situation of the sister taken as a whole is no longer congregation-orientated in character — determined, that is, by her belonging to a religious community. When it is left to her, the religious tends in fact to work in a milieu where lay people form the large majority.

The extension, among religious, of the individual salaried contract has contributed, along with community reflection and research, to a re-evaluation of the elements that constitute religious life: life in common, poverty, presence to the world and so on. It is true that the profession practised corresponds, in many cases, to the active work for which the congregation was founded: teaching, care of the sick; but increasingly it is being chosen in view of the milieu to be evangelized, from a desire to share the circumstances of others or from the necessity of providing for one's material needs. In theory one may consider that no profession is incompatible with the religious life; the choice will be made in the light of personal or community circumstances. Many young people express the wish not to leave the professional milieu in which they were living when the entered the noviciate. This tendency towards complete sharing of the living conditions of others raises another question: religious life or secular institute? Fr Beyer has warned against the possible misunderstandings that might arise from such alternative.[19] In fact it seems that we are moving in the direction of new and original formulae for an authentic form of religious life. Formerly it was impossible to imagine the apostolic religious life without some specific work; now, for many of those concerned, the activity, which will be carried out in collaboration with other men and women, is of secondary importance; what they set out to achieve is a form of life based on the Gospel which in substance is identical with the traditional understanding of the 'Come, follow me' of religious life. Paradoxically enough, this immersion in the world goes hand in hand with the search for contemplation in the context of a community; and what is asked of the religious life is not so much that it should produce great works, but that it should incarnate one of these 'spiritual spaces' where evangelical freedom is a visible reality.

(c) Here again, existing legislation often has difficulty in meeting the needs of the living situation. The presence of religious in a given place presupposed, in law, the canonical foundation of a house which must be guaranteed a certain measure of stability. Today introduction into a new environment generally begins modestly enough, with some uncertainty about the future, and sometimes anonymously. However, if religious life has a place in the Church, can such a foundation really be made completely independently, without some reference to the Christian community, diocesan or local? One understands the bishops when they claim the right to be informed as to where religious are living and what projects they are undertaking. But in the urban context it is not always possible to make stability in one place binding, constitutionally, on a community.

IV. RELEASING THE FORCES OF LIFE

The religious life is having to contend with serious liabilities. The ageing of institutes is an inexorable fact; the lack of new blood is equally disquieting. It is urgent that we should make ready for some kind of future. This can only be done by drawing on vital sources, which will have to be released according to ways and means that may not always be the traditional ones. Then life will call forth life.

The survey conducted by Luchini brought to light definite indications of health. If many institutions are dying out, new foundations are appearing in almost equal numbers. Collaboration between institutes has become an accepted fact, and inter-congregational communities are by no means rare. A relatively significant number of institutes — more in France than elsewhere, apparently — have amalgamated or made use of the provisions for federation or association set down in *Perfectae Caritatis*, 11. However. if solutions of this kind are adopted when the urgency of the situation becomes too overwhelming, they still run the risk of pushing the problems into the background without actually solving them. There is the risk, too, that vital forces may simply be used to paper over the cracks which will then get deeper; or else they will begin to feel less and less committed as far as their own institute is concerned.

Up till the present day the institute has been the unique source of stability in the religious life. Now one can imagine that the day may

come when commitment is made in the context of great spiritual movements — whether they have their origin in some long-standing spiritual
tradition or emerge from the living tissue of the contemporary Church.

This is no purely utopian dream, since already a number of concrete
examples have come to light; it is in just this way that institutes which
are spiritually akin to one another are drawing closer together. The
example of religious families attracting religious men and women (both
nuns and sisters dedicated to the apostolic life) together with lay people
gives some idea of the possible shape of things to come. Thus, instead
of entering the spiritual family directly by way of commitment to a
congregation, a Dominican or Franciscan sister would bind herself in
the first instance to the Order of St Dominic or of St Francis, the
Order being interpreted here as a charismatic entity and not as an institute for the friars alone. As far as organization is concerned, the congregation could remain very flexible, allowing for the creation of many
smaller networks within the total Dominican or Franciscan context.
Jean Isaac even insists that reciprocal ties should be formed between all
the members of a spiritual family, and that they should not be considered a prerogative of the religious: 'It is highly desirable that people
living in widely varying situations should be able to find a place within
it. Men and women, married or single, priests and lay people, those
are by temperament contemplatives and the missionaries, thinkers or
builders, listeners or doers, let all be accepted on a strictly equal basis,
and provided they have received the same call, it would change the
future.'[20] This in fact is what he sees as the means of overcoming what
he calls, with a touch of the dramatic, 'the present state of collapse'.

Looking at religious life as a whole, J. M. Tillard adopts a similar
point of view, without attempting to gloss over the far-reaching implica-
tions of the developments he foresees, since 'this dynamic of growth
may well come to the point where it severs the umbilical cords through
which links are still maintained with the original congregations, and so
bring about the birth of new and smaller groups possessing a great inner
vitality. Being fairly independent, these groups will probably feel the
need no longer to find their place within the present framework of the
large, centralized and hierarchically-structured communities, but rather
to establish among themselves a new system of communion, sharing and
solidarity which might on occasion go so far as to include interchange
of members. Some communities belonging to the Reformed Churches
are living extremely happily in just such situations.'[21]

Judging from the facts, these trends have only been realized in a
modest way as yet, but they do exist and seem — provided they develop
— to be a sign of hope for the future. Today, hope is not simply concerned with the destiny of individuals: the institutions on which we
were once able to rely with such assurance have been badly shaken and

we still do not know what the future will look like. In order to ensure the survival of the charism of religious life in the western Church, one might wonder whether, in the future, the Holy Spirit may not call on a number of existing congregations to enter into the mystery of the cross and the mysterious fruitfulness of Easter, not in order to scuttle their own vessel — which would be an act of cowardice and a sin against hope — but to allow new forms of life to be born of them, forms more in harmony with the Church's image if herself as sign and instrument of the Kingdom of God at the very heart of the new world which is emerging as part of an irreversible process; to disappear, cutting themselves off gradually from the truly living members, thus allowing for a new flowering in the Church. Acceptance of all this in faith has nothing to do with evasion of responsibility or admission of defeat. It is a matter of entering, in the spirit of the Gospel, into the radical poverty of the Lord Jesus, which always overflows into 'newness of life'.

Translated by Sarah Fawcett

Notes

1   There are in France about 19,000 male religious (including 1775 monks), about 100,000 women religious in more than 400 congregations and 350 monasteries.

2   *Leur aggiornamento* (Lyon, 1970).

3   J. Beyer SJ, 'Premier bilan des chapitres de renouveau', in *Nouvelle Revue Théologique*, 95 (1973), pp. 60-86.

4   Regular reports in *La Revue des Sciences Philosophiques et Théologiques, La Revue Thomiste, Vie Consacrée*.

5   By way of example, compare O. du Roy, 'L'avenir de la vie religieuse', in *Esprit*, 408 (1971), pp. 736-46, with P. R. Régamey, *La Voix de Dieu dans les voix du temps* (Paris, 1973).

6   J. M. Tillard, 'Religieuses dans l'Eglise d'aujourd'hui' (Paris, 1971); the text was reprinted in *Etre religieux aujourd'hui*, Acta of the Assembly of the USMF (Paris, 1973).

7   Three volumes have appeared in A. Luchini, *Les Religieuses en France* (Paris, 1971).

8   J. M. Tillard, 'La Communauté religieuse', in *Nouvelle Revue Théologique*, 94 (1972), pp. 488-519; 95 (1973), pp. 150-87.

9   'Religieux, danse la societé nouvelle', in *Lumen Vitae*, XXVIII (1973), pp. 274.

10   P. Maillard, 'N'éteignez pas l'Esprit', in *Christus* 80, pp. 451-63.

11   J. Isaac, 'Réévaluer les voeux' (Paris, 1973).

12   Habitations à Loyer Modéré (low-rent accommodation).

13   *loc. cit.*, p. 169.

14   *loc. cit.*

15   Marie le Roy Ladurie, *Femmes au desert* (Paris, 1971).

16   J. M. Tillard, *Qu'attend l'Eglise de la vie contemplative?* (Paris, 1973).

17   B. Besret, *Liberation de l'homme* (Paris, 1969); O. du Roy, *Moines d'aujourd'hui* (Paris, 1972).
18   P. Raffin, 'Reveils spirituels et rénovation dans la vie religieuse', in *Concilium* 89, p. 52.
19   J. Isaac, *loc. cit.*, p. 212.
20   J. M. Tillard, 'Religieux dans la societé nouvelle', *loc. cit.*, p. 282.
21   *Ibid.*

Agnes Cunningham

Appropriate Renewal and Ecclesial Identity

NEARLY ten years have passed since religious were summoned to the appropriate renewal[1] of their state of life by the documents of Vatican II.[2] During this time, much confusion and uncertainty have prevailed. To many religious, the project of renewal has seemed unclear. This is so, despite the fact that religious life has been called a special manner of following the universal call to holiness within the *ekklesia*;[3] a means by which Christians, both clerical and lay, are joined 'to the Church and her mystery in a special way';[4] a state of life which 'belongs inseparably' to the life of the Church'.[5]

In an attempt to renew and adapt in an appropriate manner, religious have had the courage to ask difficult questions: What does it mean to be a religious today? What are the essential characteristics of religious life in the Church? Is there a unique role for religious in the Christian community? Does the Church still need religious? Does religious life have a future?

Efforts to answer these questions have led some religious to arrive at conclusions such as those reflected in a study published in the United States in 1973.[6] Between 1965 and 1972, the average yearly decrease of membership in religious communities was 3,841.[7] Of this number, approximately 1,346 were due to deaths; 1,551 to dispensations of perpetual vows; 944, to termination of temporary vows. The year 1970 was marked by the greatest number of dispensations (2,456). Of those young women (13,476) who entered religious communities between 1965 and 1971, 5,907 remained at the time the study was made.

Statistics and their interpretations have been known to be ambiguous. Nevertheless, the fact of decreased numbers in religious life cannot be denied. Are we to conclude then, that efforts towards appropriate renewal have resulted in the undermining of religious life? Indeed, there are those who would claim that 'adaptation' has been too hasty and 'renewal', consequently, inappropriate. Or, shall we evaluate the data as so many signs that the project has failed because it was not implemented quickly enough or fully enough? Without a doubt, many would argue that too great an emphasis on 'renewal' has limited our vision of needed 'adaptation'. Again, others would read the decreased membership in religious life as a sociological factor which augurs ill for the future of the institutional Church.[8]

There us another perspective from which the phenomenon can be addressed. In recent years, religious life has been characterized by several movements which seem to express appropriate renewal, as much as they foster it. These movements are: the transition from a concept of *apostolate* to one of *ministry*; the development of the idea of *prayers as spiritual exercises* to that of *prayer as contemplation*; the trend from the ideal of *life in common* to the goal of *community*.

These movements are related to what emerges as the core issue in religious life today, namely, *ecclesial identity*. This is particularly so in the experience of religious women in the United States. An examination of and a reflection on this experience will not be out of place in an assessment of the efforts of religious to renew in fidelity the essential values of their life, even as they strive to adapt with creativity the modes by which these values are transmitted.

I. FROM APOSTOLATE TO MINISTRY[9]

The 'apostolic life' is that form of the religious life by which individuals 'are consecrated to the apostolate in its essential mission'.[10] This mission consists in 'the proclaiming of the Word of God to those whom he places along their paths, so as to lead them towards faith'. Historically speaking, the apostolic life has existed in religious 'families', founded for the purpose of 'proclaiming the Word' in the language of specific works: evangelization, education, care of the sick, service of the poor and the unfortunate.

As religious congregations and institutes came into existence in response to new needs in every age, their apostolic character became each community's *raison d'être*. In other words, one of the identifying marks of a congregation was the apostolate of the particular congregation. In time, the apostolic commitment of a religious group assumed a significant priority. Norms and criteria for membership, as for spiritual and professional preparation, were determined in reference to this priority. Increased calls for apostolic service encouraged religious communities to augment within themselves the resources necessary for response to these appeals. Slowly, religious life began to develop independently of the mainstream of the life of the Church. An 'excessively individualistic theology of the religious life'[11] came to be established.

Vatican II recognized the need for communities to preserve their unique character and purpose.[12] Religious were encouraged to return to their sources: Scripture and the charism of their founders. The revitalization of an original inspiration, at times, led to newly-perceived goals and objectives. At the same time, re-examination of government[13] brought about the introduction of new structures, such as co-responsibility and respect for the competence and potential of the individual in the assignment of apostolic undertakings. There were new insights into a 'ministry of service' to which all the People of God are called.[14] In the secular sphere, the emancipation of women was recognized as one of the 'signs of the times',[15] pointing to a new understanding of the role of women in the Church.

Against this background, the phenomenon of pastoral ministry emerged. A certain disenchantment with the past gave way to an impetus for new modes of service. By 1972, a national convention could be sponsored by the National Assembly of Women Religious on 'Women in Ministry'. This theme dealt with a two-fold *de facto* reality: ecclesial services, progressively perceived as ministries, to complement ministerial priesthood; religious women actively engaged in services where, previously, only priests had been found.

The presence of religious women in ministry, like the phenomenon of Pastoral Ministry itself, seems to have occurred prior to explicit ecclesiastical 'institution'. Religious women were among the first to perceive and to respond to new needs in a new era, often in parochial or diocesan structures, previously closed to them. As official recognition and acceptance grew, religious began to be aware of a change in their attitude toward the Church, as community and institution.

II. FROM SPIRITUAL EXERCISE TO CONTEMPLATION

The attitude of religious toward the Church was influenced by a second movement: development of the idea of prayer. The transition from apostolate to ministry oriented religious to a wider sphere of activity and vision in lives of service. Development in prayer led more deeply into personal integration.

It was certainly not impossible to lead a life of deep, interior, personal prayer within the context of community prayer, in the past. However, it was increasingly difficult to do so as professional and social obligations of religious increased. A quickened life-pace, along with multiplied pressures heightened the need for greater interior solitude, felt by many religious before they were able to articulate this concern.

Vatican II called religious to a renewal of the spirit and practice of prayer.[16] Greater flexibility in the *horarium* resulted in fewer *prayers* 'in common' and a wider personal choice of times and places for more reflective, meditative prayer.

The transition from a former mode of religious community prayer to one that favoured stronger personal initiative was not uneventful. It was difficult to remember a schedule announced previously by bells. It was not always easy to maintain motivation for an activity previously shared and supported by the presence of others. Absence of an earlier doctrinal formation might manifest itself in a crisis intensified by echoes and overtones of the 'death of God' theology.

There was too much sincerity and anguish in this search for renewal in prayer to fail. In time, persons and places were found to encourage and foster efforts toward openness to the Word of God and response to the Spirit of the Lord. Houses of prayer, directed retreats, spiritual discernment, the charismatic movement — these went hand-in-hand with internalized values derived from personalism and the communication skills. Religious learned to share their spiritual experiences, their faith-life, their quest for God more fully. From there, it was but a step to the recognition that every Christian is called to that worship of God 'in spirit and truth' (Jn. 4.23) which constitutes the heart of contemplative prayer. Prayer as contemplation must be combined with apostolic love for the sake of the Kingdom.[17] Today, prayer — personal, communal, shared or liturgical — is one of the most vital aspects of religious life. It is a sign of renewal that is not always clearly read.

III. FROM LIFE-IN-COMMON TO COMMUNITY

The transition from community-based apostolates to ecclesial ministries and from a predominantly communitarian prayer to prayer as a factor of personal integration might have posed a threat to one of the essential values of religious life. However, a third movement helped to provide needed balance in a transition from life-in-common to community, perceived in a new dimension as a human and a Christian value.

The stress on unity through uniformity in the external signs associated with religious life throughout its historical evolution had been a source of strength and identity in the experience of many religious. The need to preserve the initial inspiration of a charismatic founder often led to a structure of customs envisioned as fundamental traditions. The return to essentials evoked by Vatican II provoked a healthy distance from which to evaluate situations too long invested with significance beyond their cultural moment. The ancient Christian principle of *unity in diversity* suggests other ways in which fraternal life for the sake of the Kingdom may be lived.

In this perspective, for example, it is possible to conceive of the life-situation of religious in terms of *qualitative* rather than *quantitative* presence. Simplicity, joy and hospitality are human and Christian virtues which facilitate corporate witness to the Holy, as well as mutual sharing in friendship of celibate love, evangelical poverty and obedience in response to the service of authority.[18] A more dynamic understanding of Christian perfection in regard to a common rule of life has enabled religious to grow in understanding of their own human limitattions and those of others. They have learned to be more realistic about the demands of community — what can be expected from it, what must be brought to it. They have been able to accept the challenge of community as a goal ever to be built.

Community, as differentiated from life-in-common, is based on a search for and an experience of Christian love (*agape*). It presupposes the willingness to promote reverence for persons through interpersonal relations and effective communication. The transition to community has brought about a renewed appreciation of religious life as *ecclesiola*. In a community of faith and love, religious are to be to the Church what the Church is to be to the world.[19]

IV. ECCLESIAL IDENTITY

It is only through reflection on the transition toward ministry, contemplation and community that ecclesial identity can be discerned as the core issue in religious life today. Many religious themselves would be reluctant to admit this. This reluctance is due, in part, to a negative experience of Church in matters of appropriate renewal since Vatican II.

Because they have often experienced the Church as an authoritarian, ecclesiastical institution, some religious have challenged the principle of their canonical status. Because they have experienced tension and strain in certain relationships with the Church, religious have attempted to live religious life without the Church. Religious have known frustration because of ecclesiastical indifference in matters of importance. They have known anger, when issues have been treated as values. Despite all this, they seek nothing more than to be women of the Church whose contribution is recognized and welcomed.

This fundamental desire for ecclesial identity results from an experience of the mystery of the Church in the practical order. Religious have shared in the *diakonia* of the Church through ministries of service; in the reality of the Church as *ecclesia orans*; in the *koinonia* of the Church as a community of faith. Through reflection on their ecclesial identity, religious will arrive at a more adequate integration of experience with articulated consciousness. In the last analysis, the ability of religious to accept the challenge to confront the issue of their ecclesial identity in this manner may be the most adequate assessment of the past ten years and the most reassuring statement for the future of religious life in the Church.

Notes

1   The Latin phrase, *De accommodata renovatione*, is more commonly referred to as, 'renewal and adaptation'.

2   Cf. *Lumen Gentium* VI (subsequently, LG), 'The Dogmatic Constitution on the Church' (21 November, 1964), in *The Documents of Vatican II*, Walter A. Abbott, S.J. (ed.) (New York, 1966); also, *Perfectae Caritatis* (subsequently, PC), 'Decree of the Appropriate Renewal of the Religious Life' (28 October, 1965).

3   Cf. LG; Abbott, *op. cit.*, n. 207, p. 43.

4   LG, 44; also, cf. 43.

5   LG, 44.

6   *A Study on Entrances and Departures in Religious Communities of Women in the United States 1965-1972*, conducted by Sister Margaret Modde, O.S.F., director of the National Sisters Vocation Conference. A report of this study can be found in the *1974 Catholic Almanac*, Felician A. Foy, O.F.M. (ed.) (Huntington, Indiana), pp. 570-1. 'Study findings were based on data supplied by 274 participating communities with a membership of 103,014. (The total number of religious communities of women in the U.S. in 1972 was approximately 455, with an overall membership of 145,000.)'

7   These and the following figures refer only to data submitted by communities participating in the study referred to above.

8   Figures from the National Opinion Research Centre, Chicago, Illinois, point to a decline in church attendance among Roman Catholics in general.

9   For a discussion of this phenomenon, cf. *Women in Ministry*, Ethne Kennedy (ed.) (Chicago, 1972).

10   *Evangelica Testificatio* (subsequently, ET), Apostolic Exhortation of Pope Paul VI (29 June, 1971), 9.

11   Abbott, *op. cit.*, n. 215, p. 75.

12   Cf. PC, 2b.

13   *Ibid.*, 3.

14   *Ibid.*, 1.

15   *Apostolicam Actuositatem*, 'Decree on the Apostolate of the Laity' (18 November, 1965); Abbott, *op. cit.*, 10, p. 500.

16   PC, 3.

17   *Ibid.*, 10.

18   *Ibid.*, 39.

19   LG, 31.

CONTRIBUTORS

WALTER DIRKS is a Doctor of Theology of the University of Münster, and Honorary Professor of the Land Nordrhein-Westfalen in the Federal Republic of Germany. A well-known journalist and writer.

The late DAVID KNOWLES was Regius Professor Emeritus of Modern History in the University of Cambridge, England, and a leading historian of western monasticism.

HANS KRAMER teaches moral theology at the University of Münster in the Federal Republic of Germany and is author of several works on the subject.

AQUINATA BÖCKMANN OSB is Reader in Moral Theology at the Papal Institute Regina Mundi.

GHISLAIN LAFONT teaches dogmatic theology at the Abbaye Saine Marie de le Pierre qui Vire in France and is the author of several works on the subject.

TARSICIUS JAN VAN BAVEL OSA is the President of the Theological Commission for Religious in Belgium and Director of the Augustine Historical Institute in Heverlee.

JEAN BEYER SJ is former Professor of Moral Theology and Law at Louvain and teaches at the Gregorian University. He has published several works on the religious life.

ROBERT SOULLARD OP teaches at the faculty of Catholic Theology in Lyons.

AGNES CUNNINGHAM SSCM is a Doctor of Sacred Theology (Lyons), has been researching at the Catholic University of America and is the author of many theological articles.